when this key sketch gets real
tongue is fork hen is cock
when this key sketch gets real
my baby eagle's dream comes true

drawings by Natesh

BLAFT
PUBLICATIONS
PRIVATE LIMITED

First published in India in 2008 by
Blaft Publications Pvt. Ltd.

ISBN 978 81 906056 2 5

Blaft Publications Pvt. Ltd.
#27 Lingam Complex
Dhandeeswaram Main Road
Velachery
Chennai 600042
email: blaft@blaft.com

Printed at
Sudarshan Graphics, Chennai

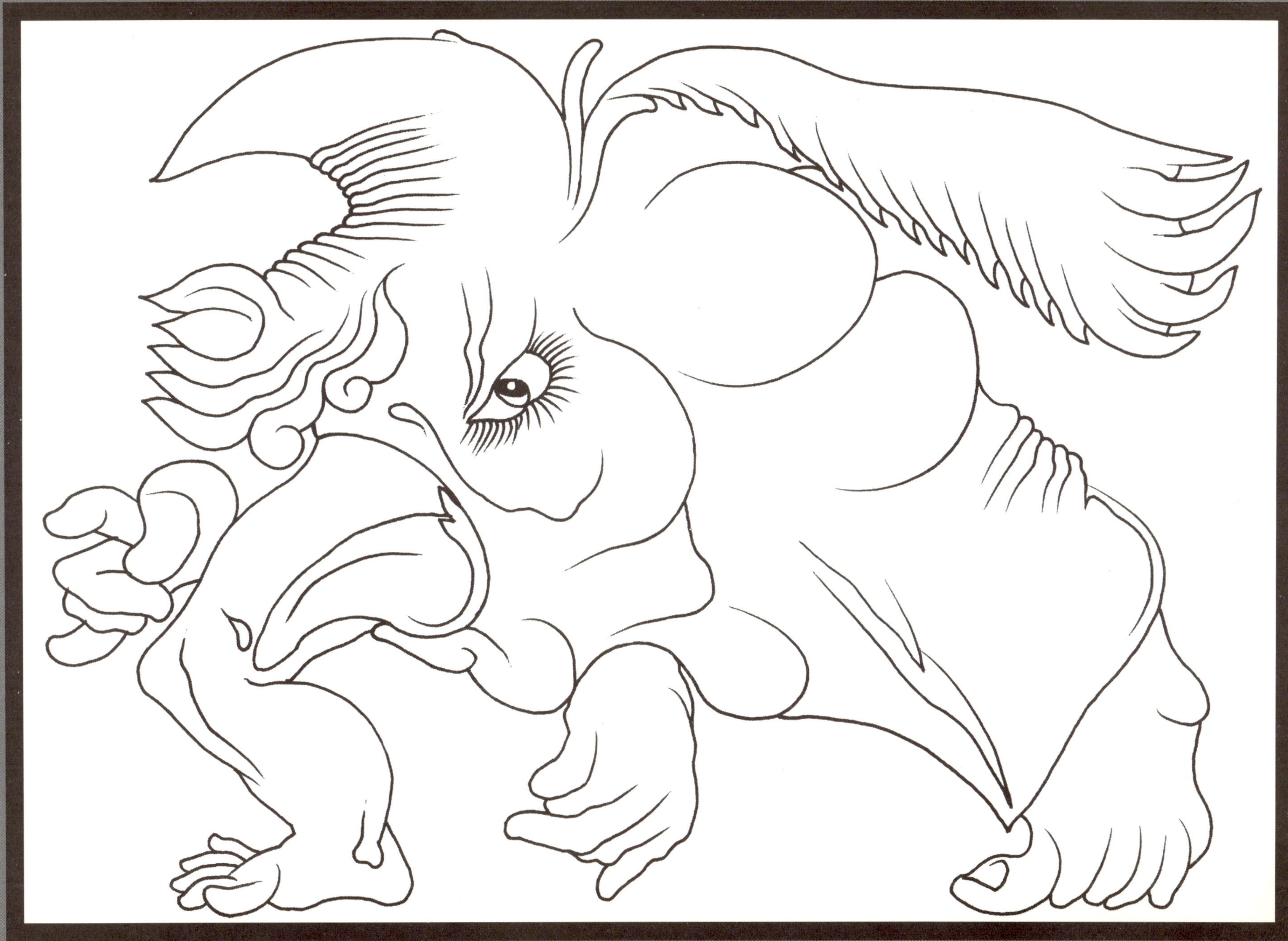

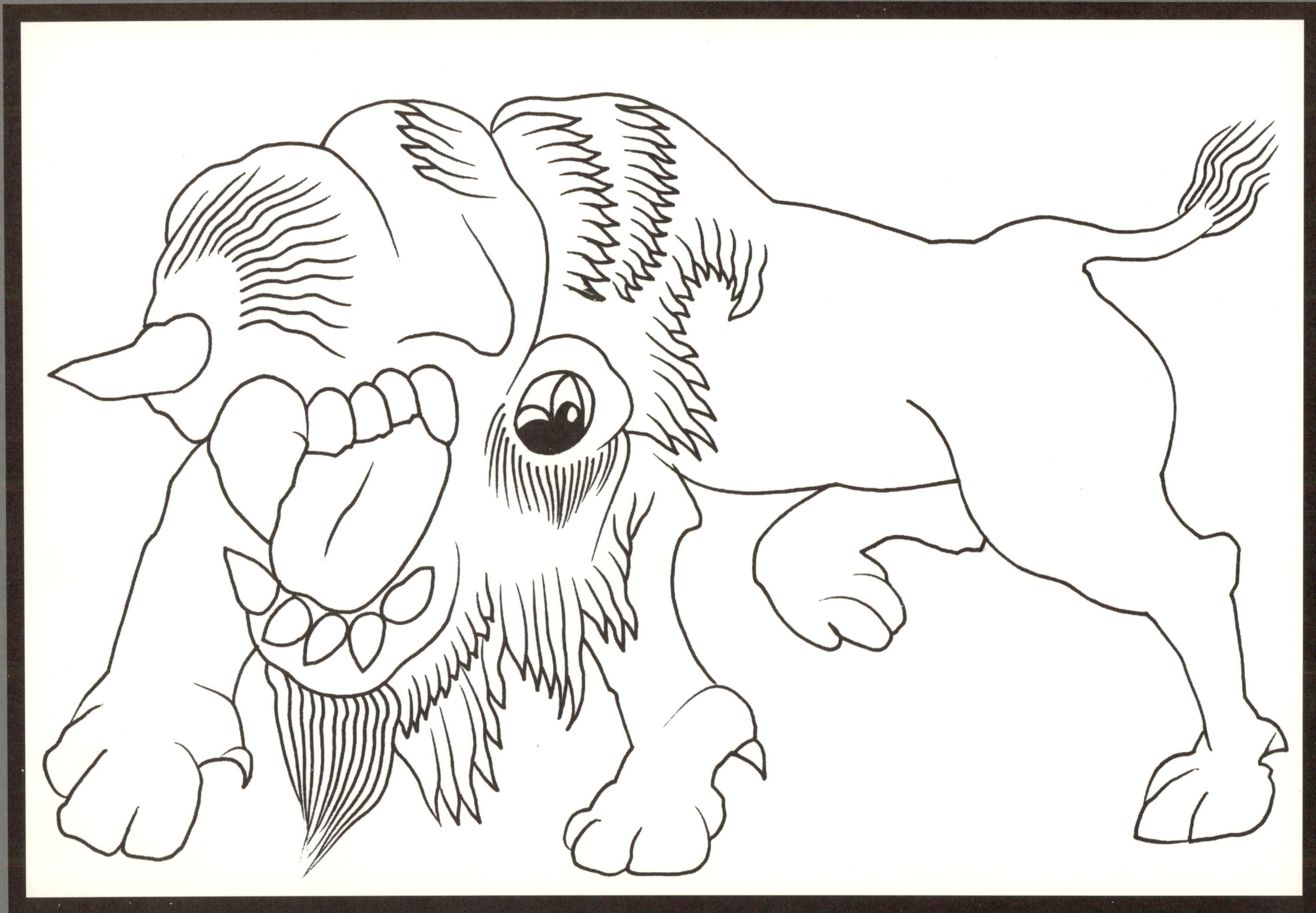

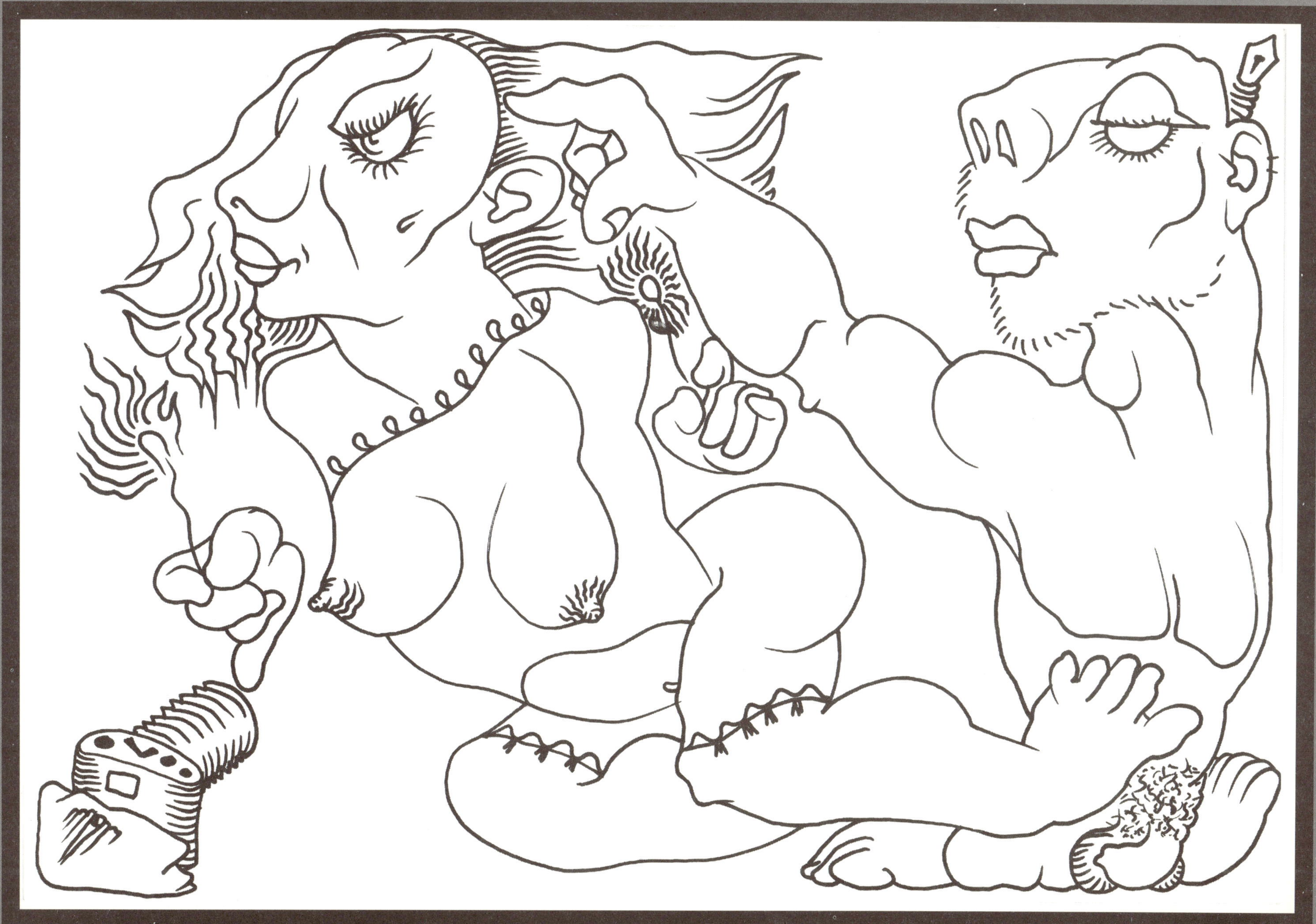

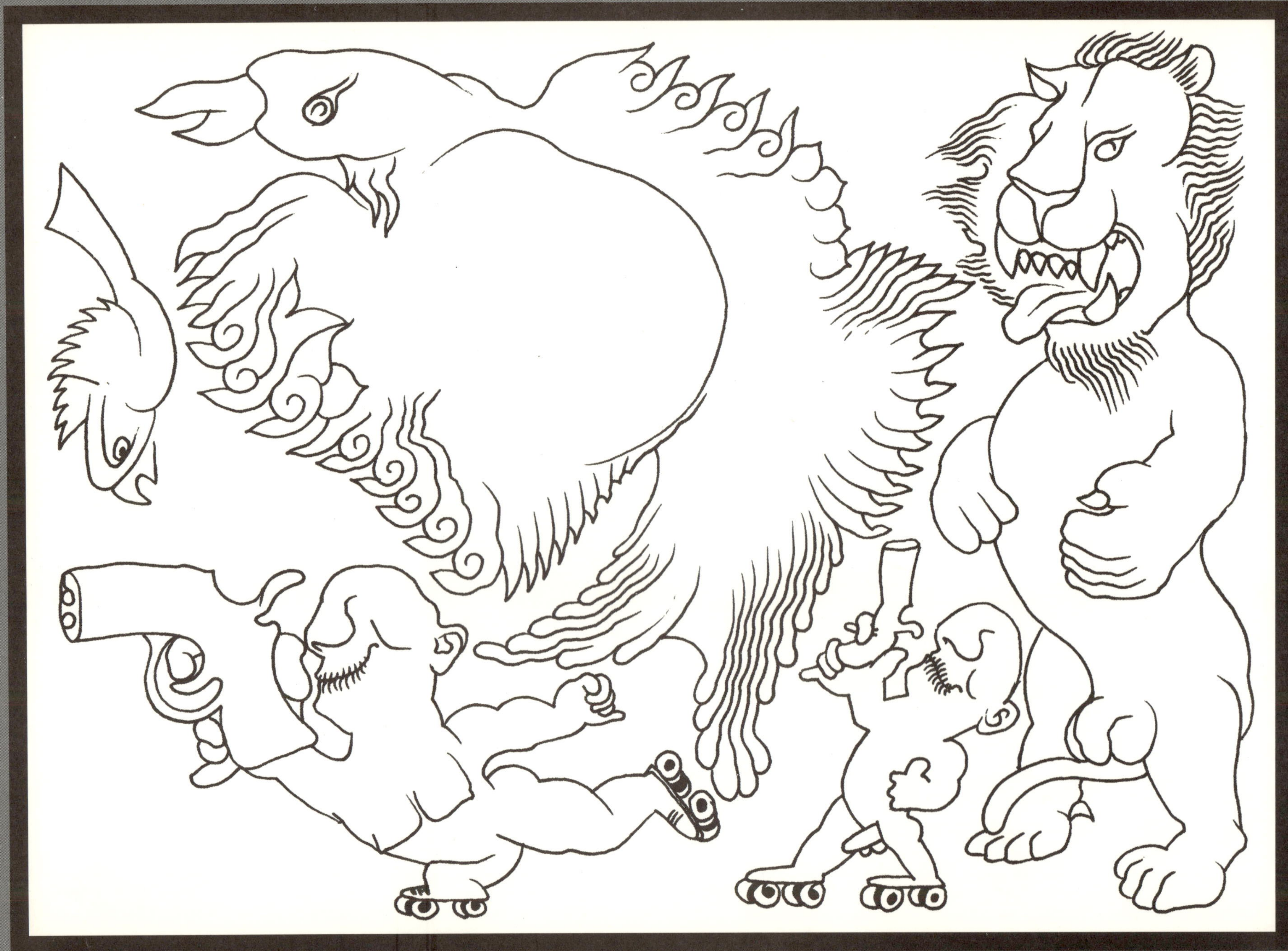

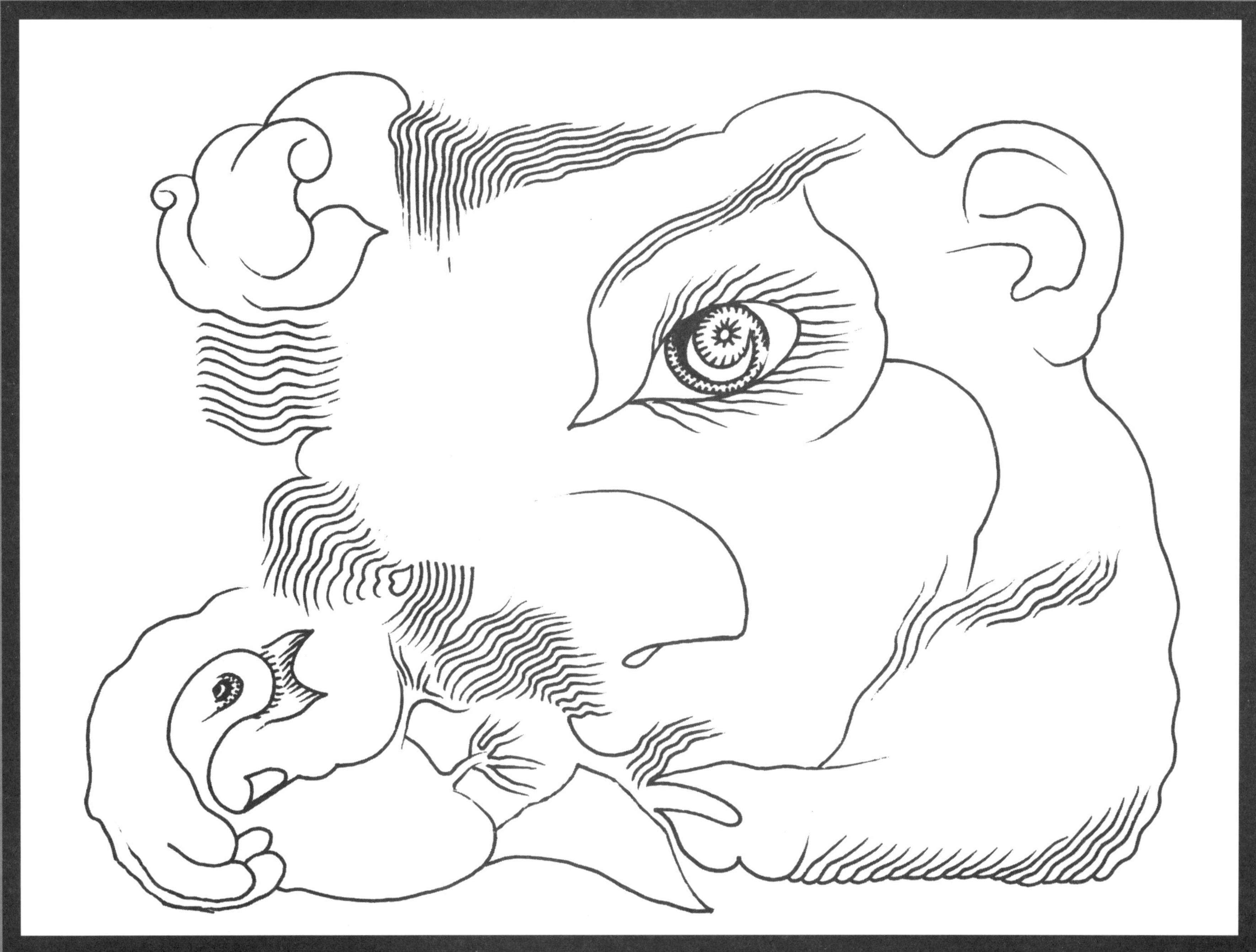

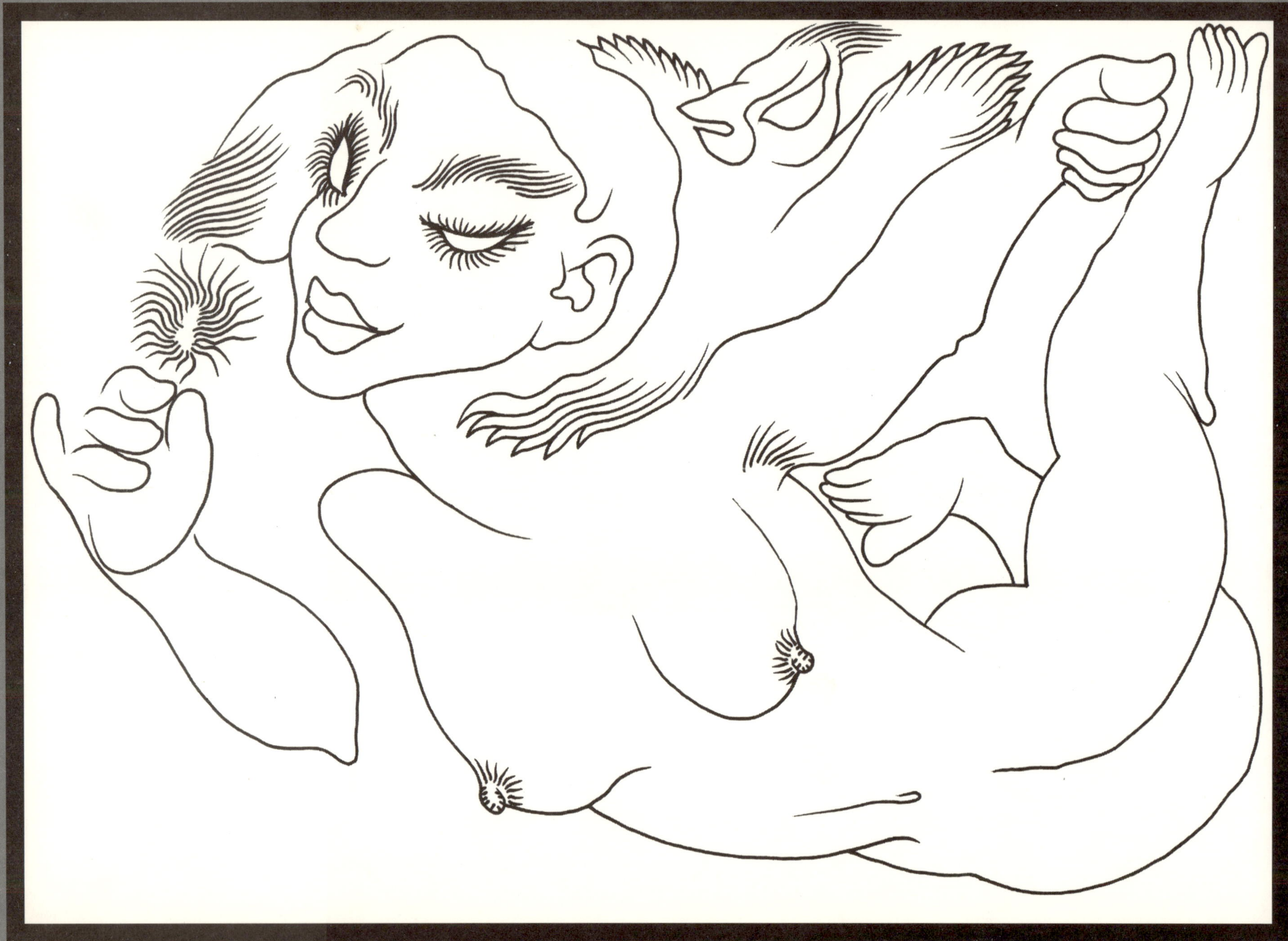

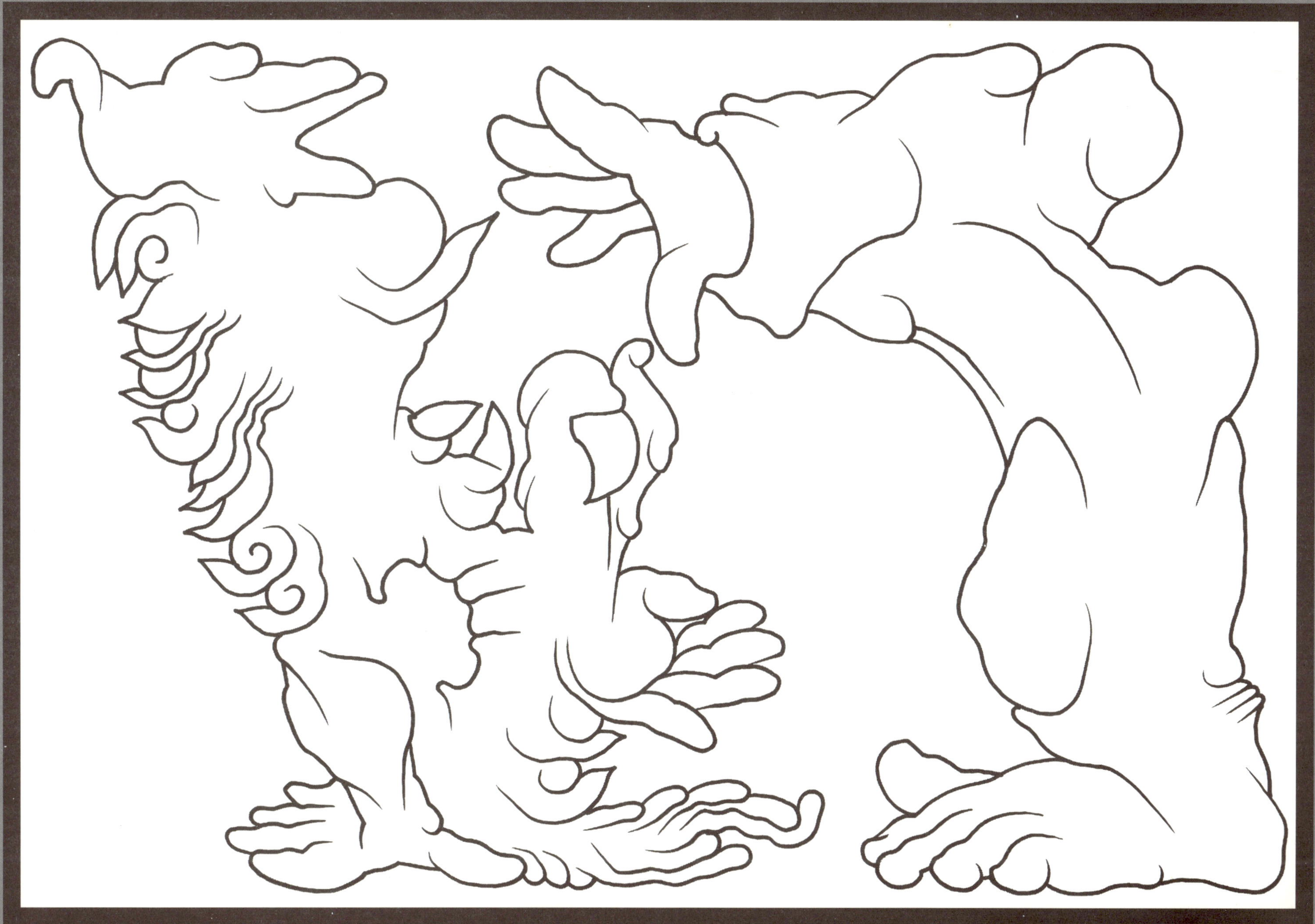

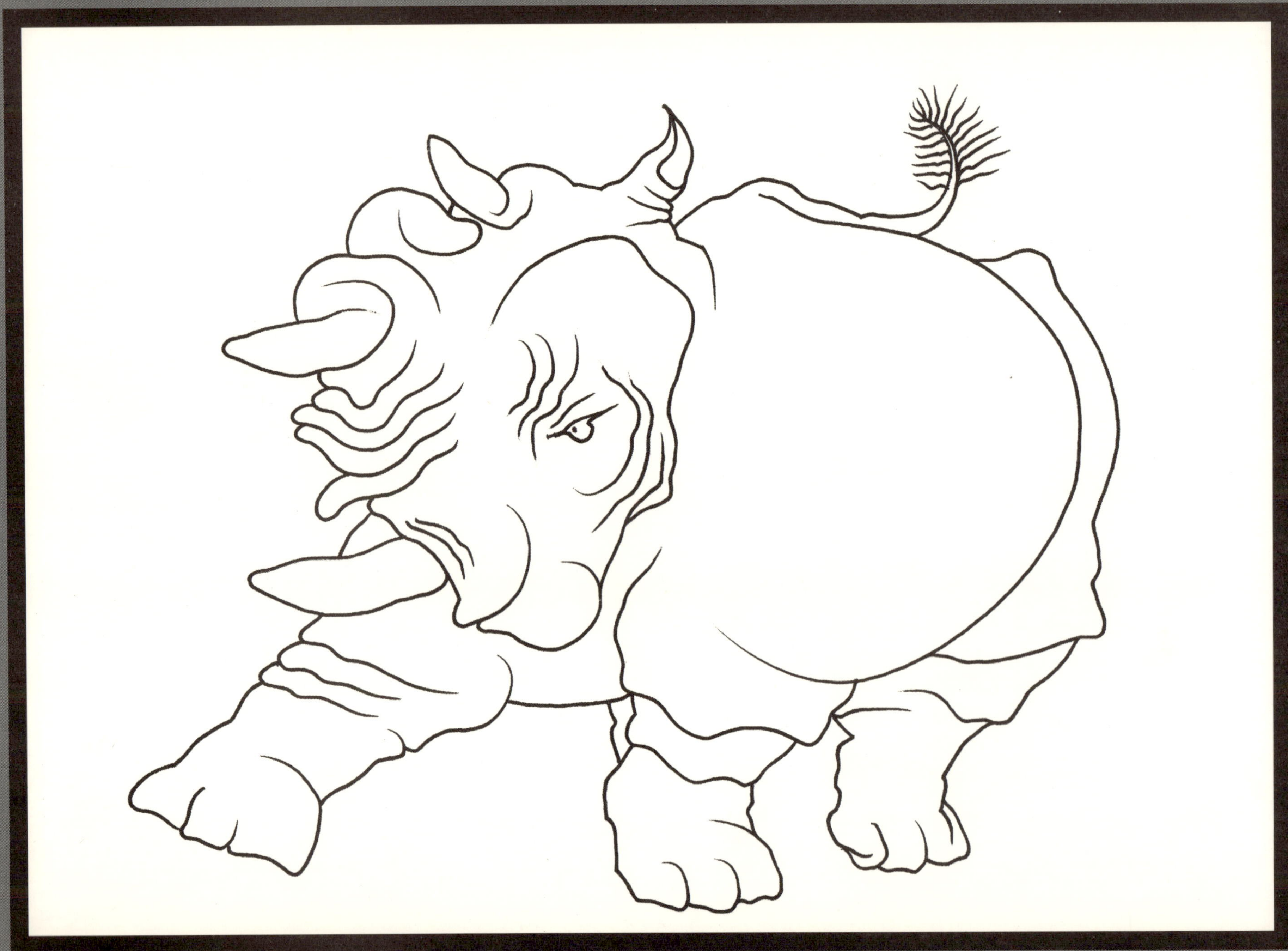

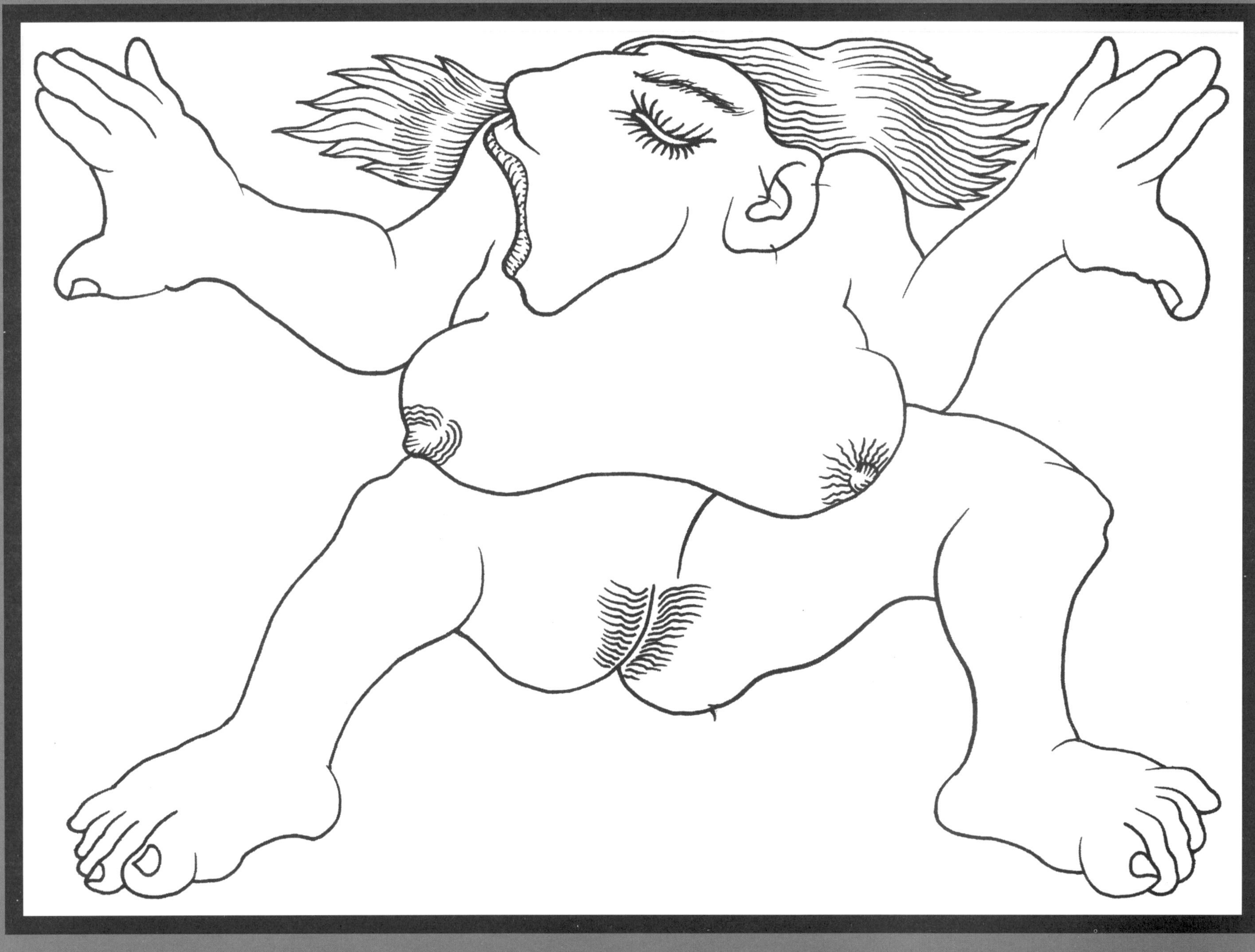

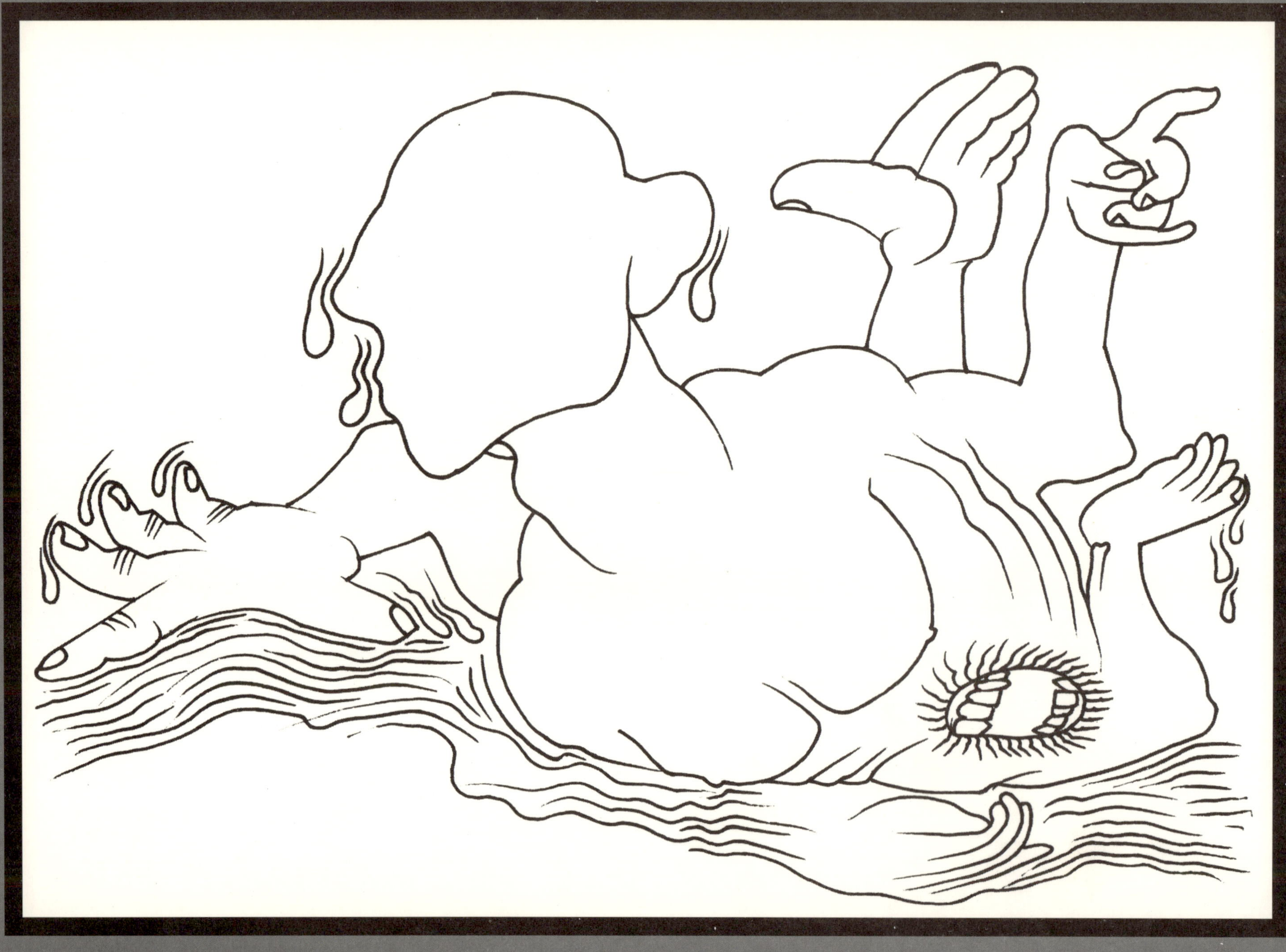

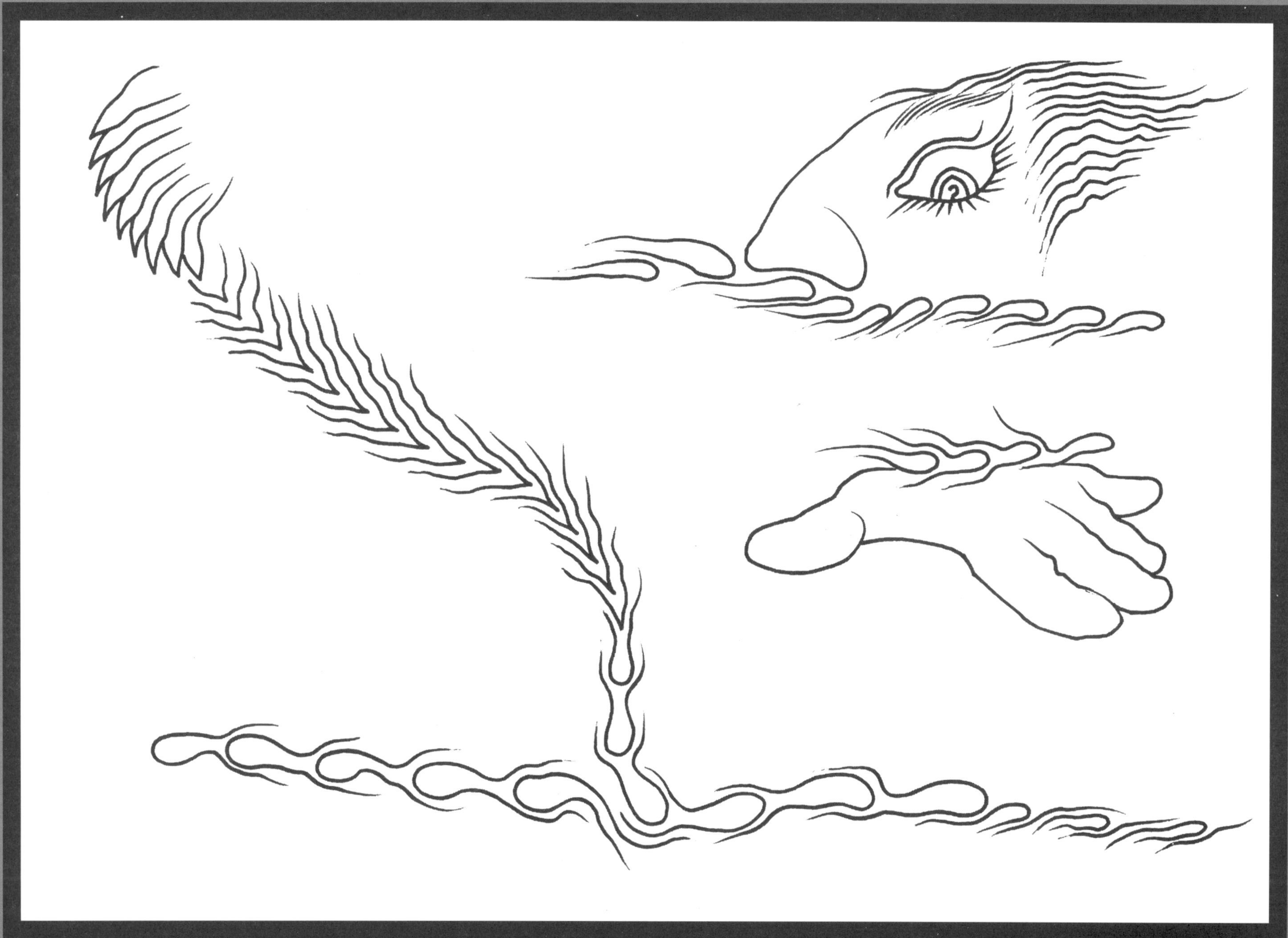

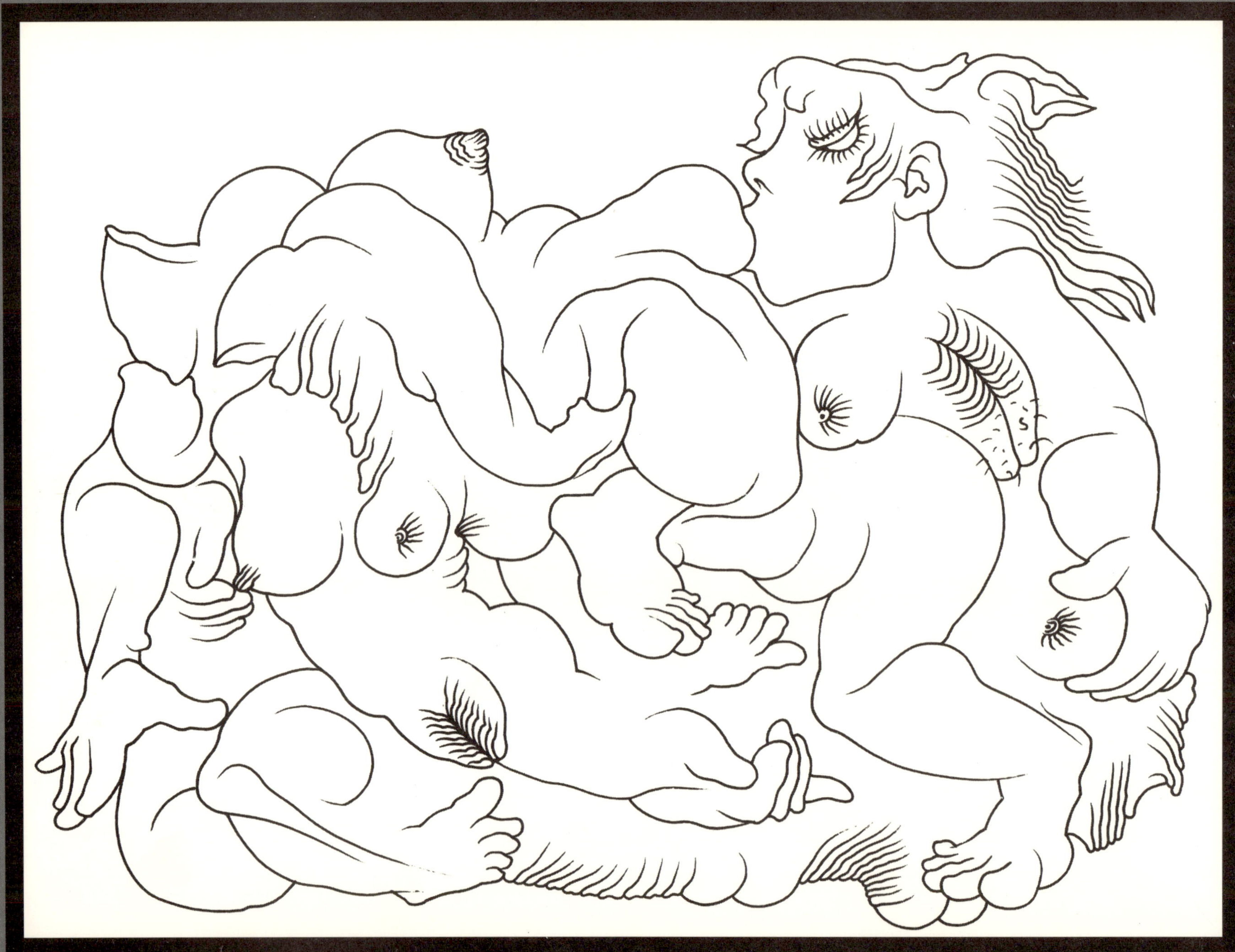

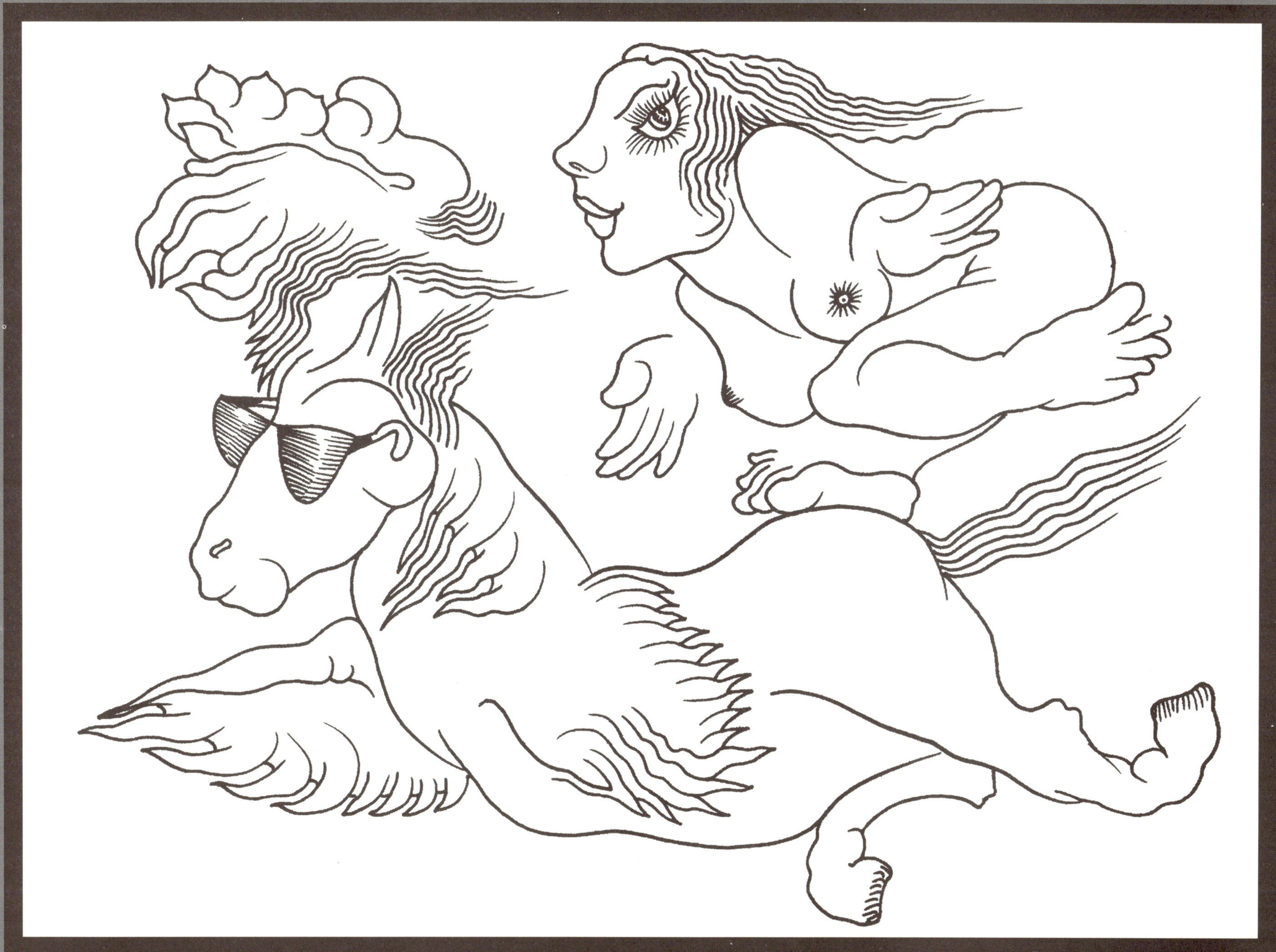

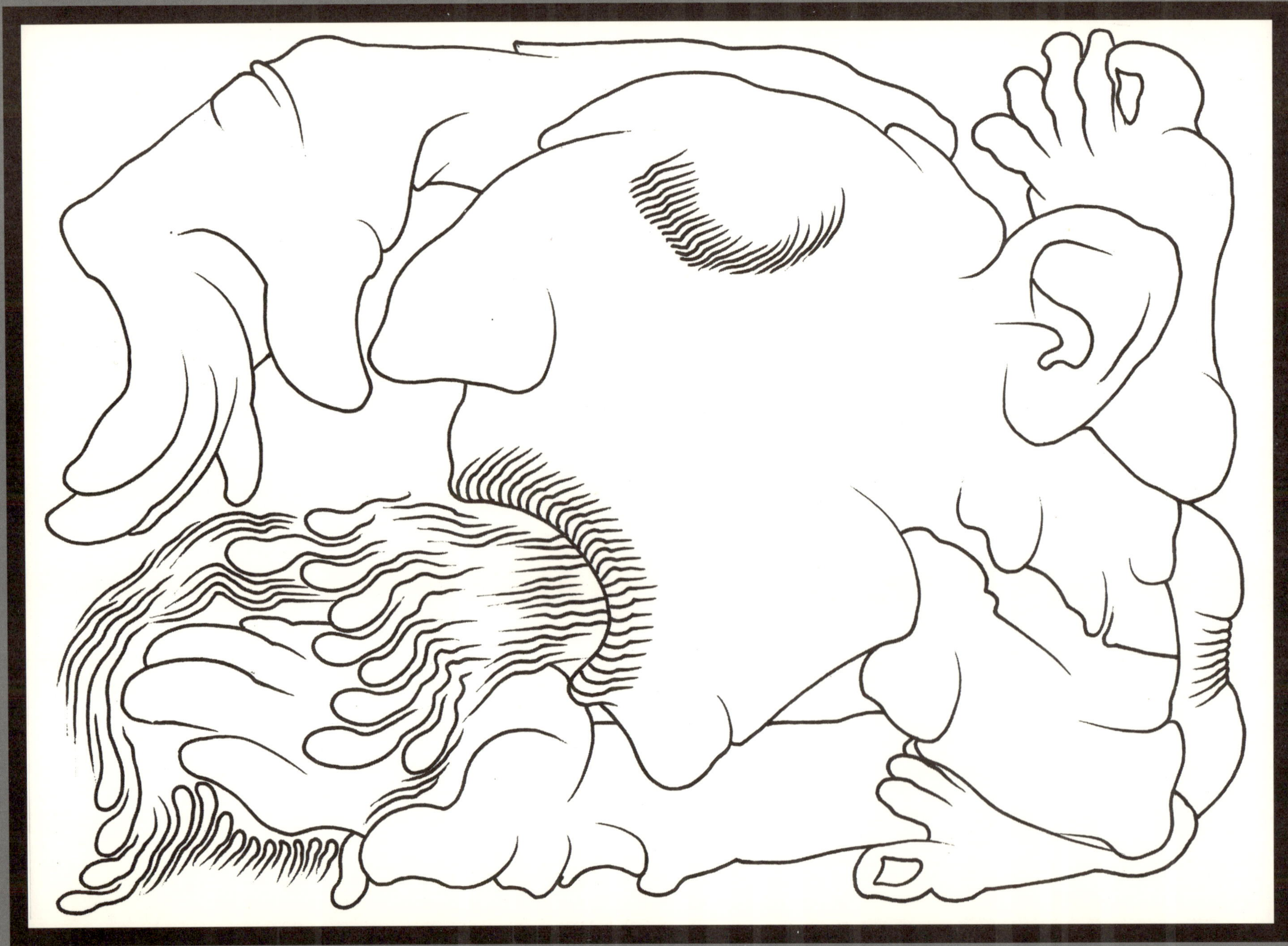

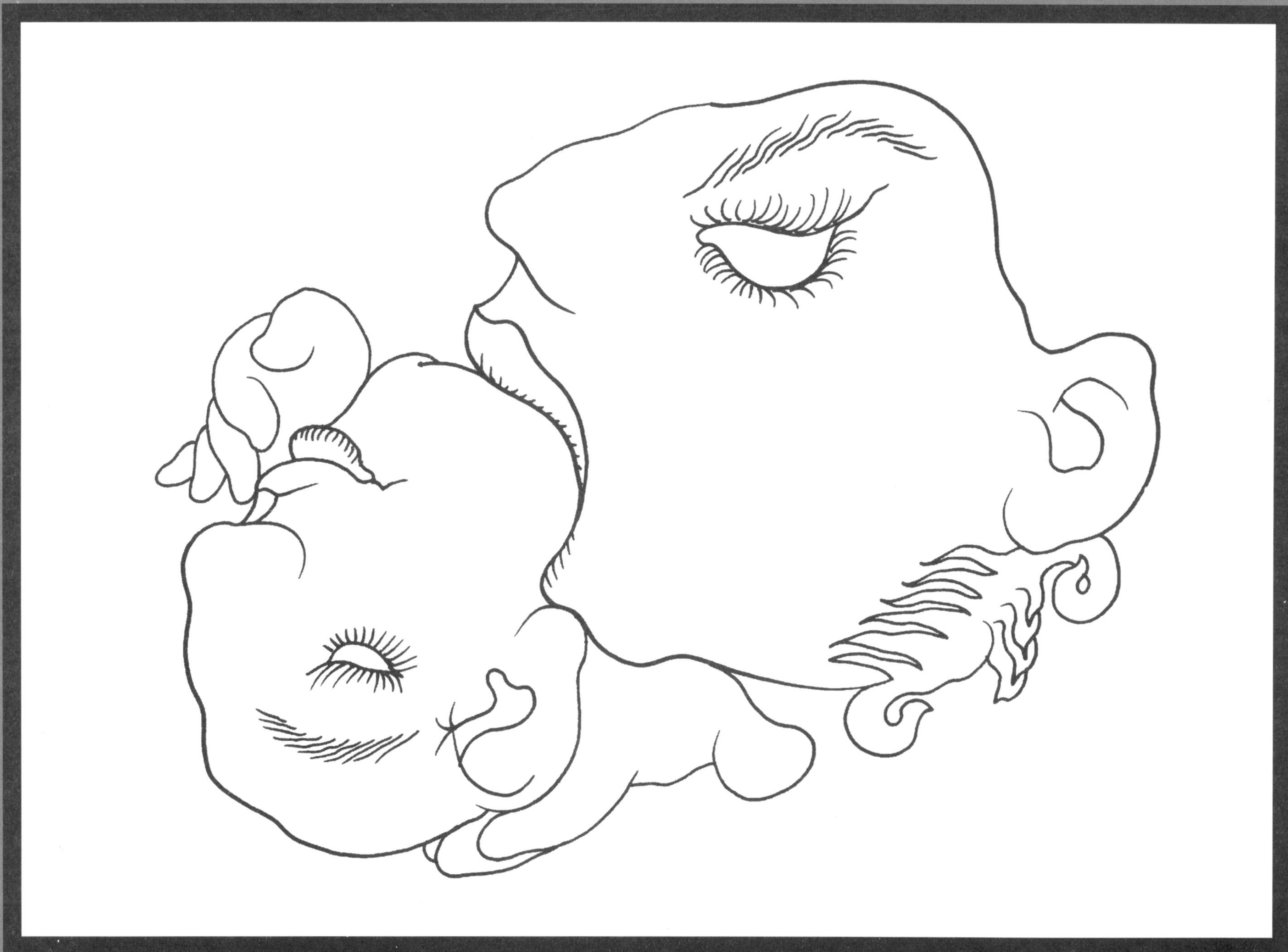

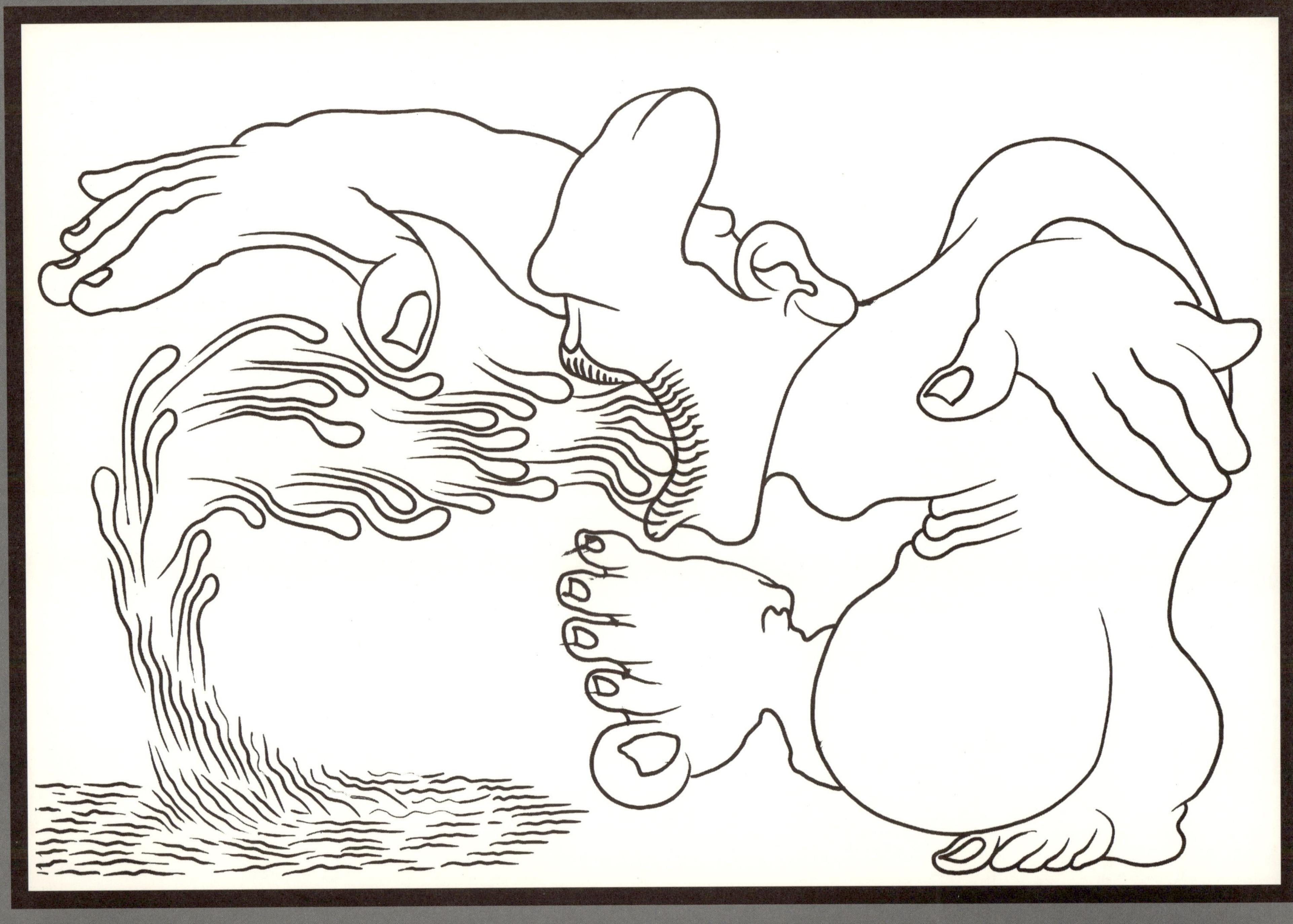

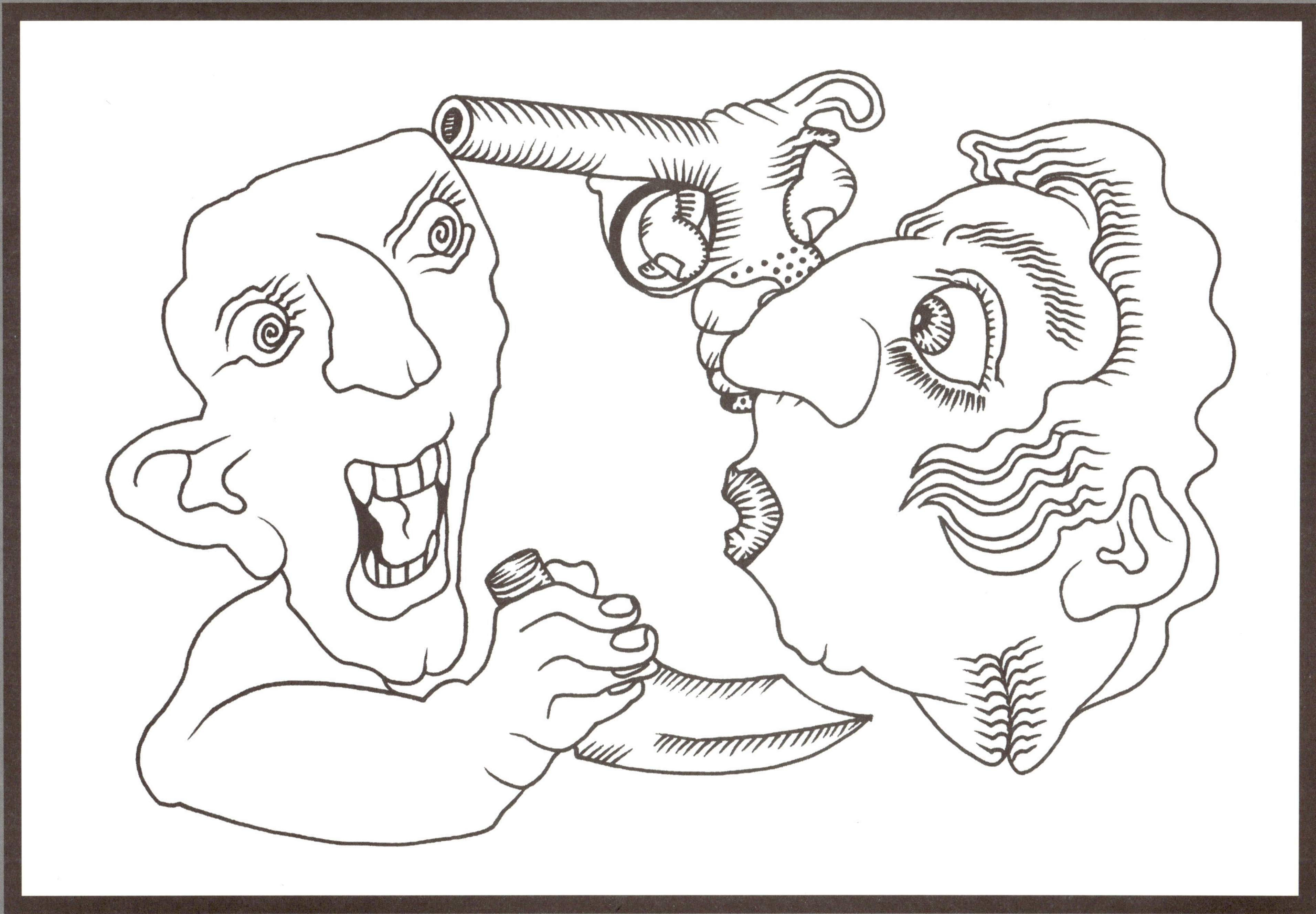

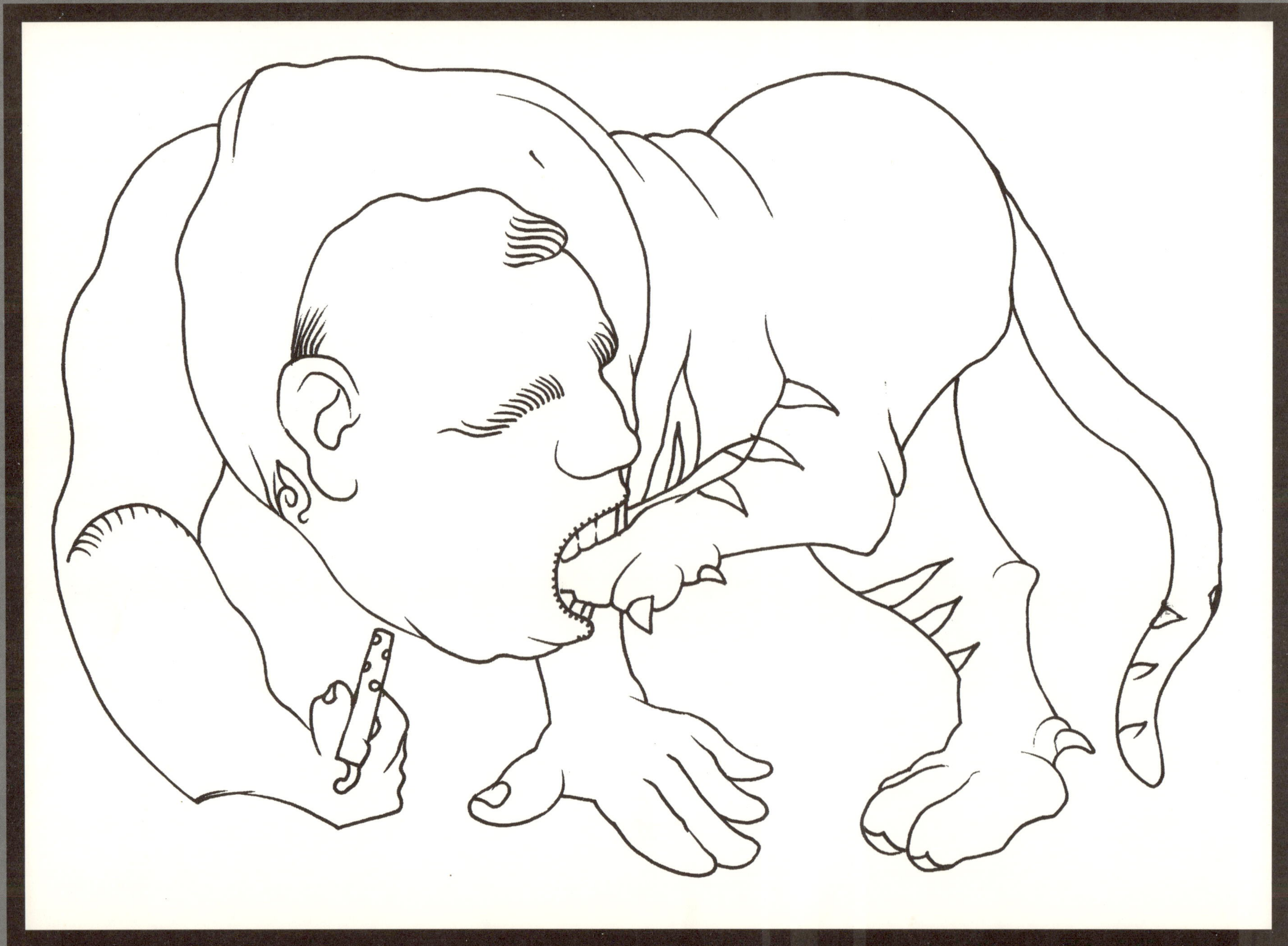

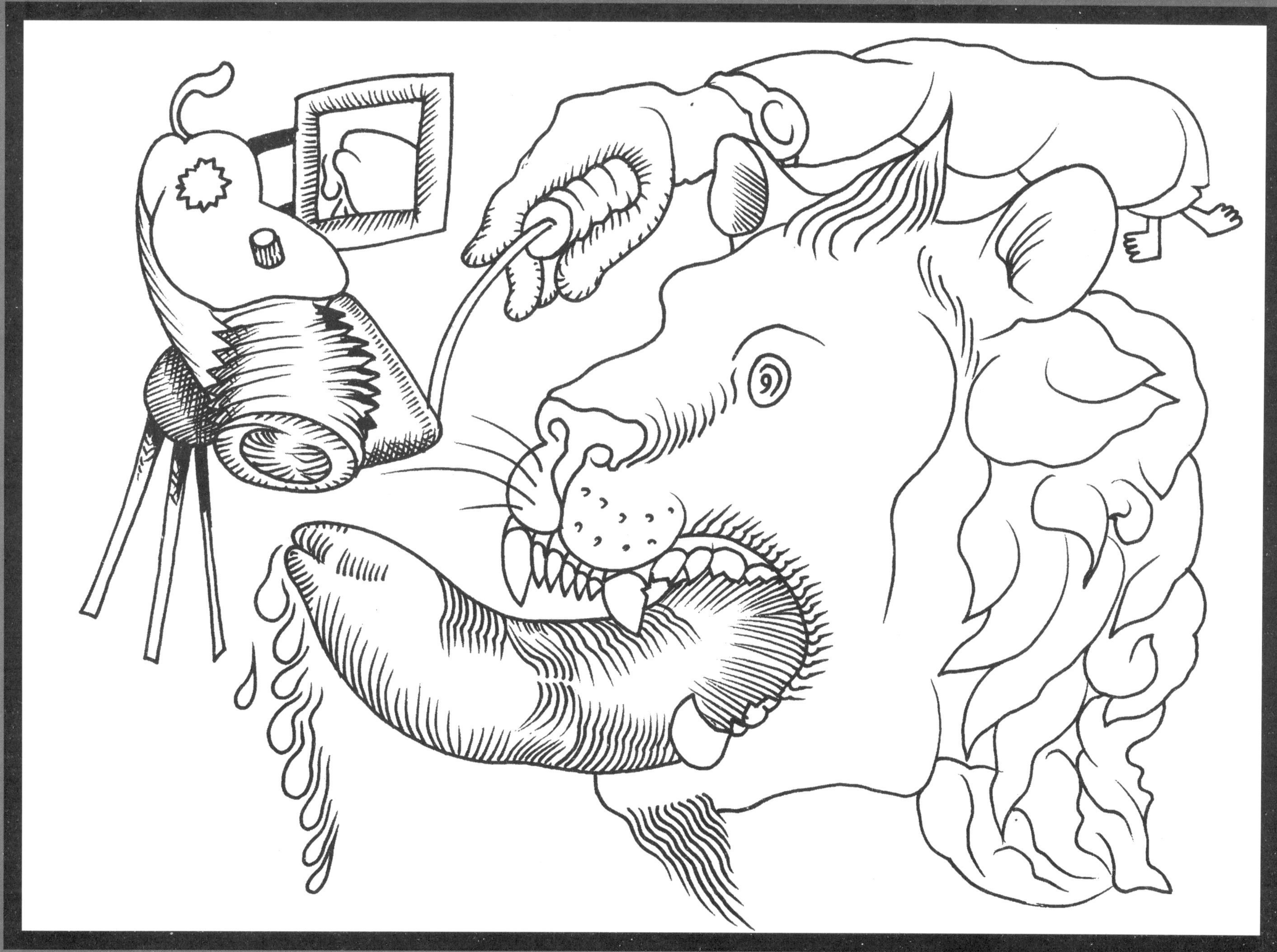

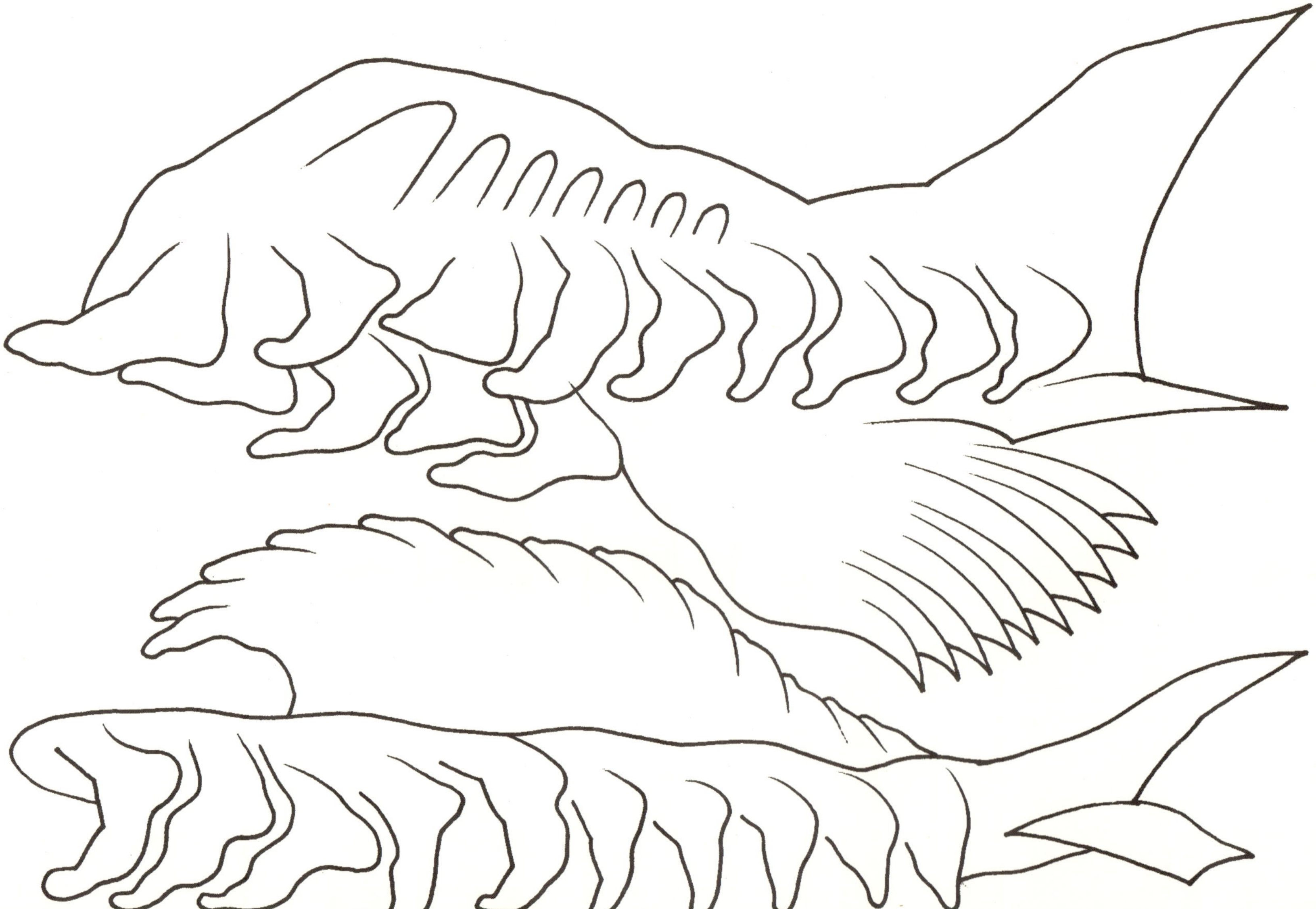

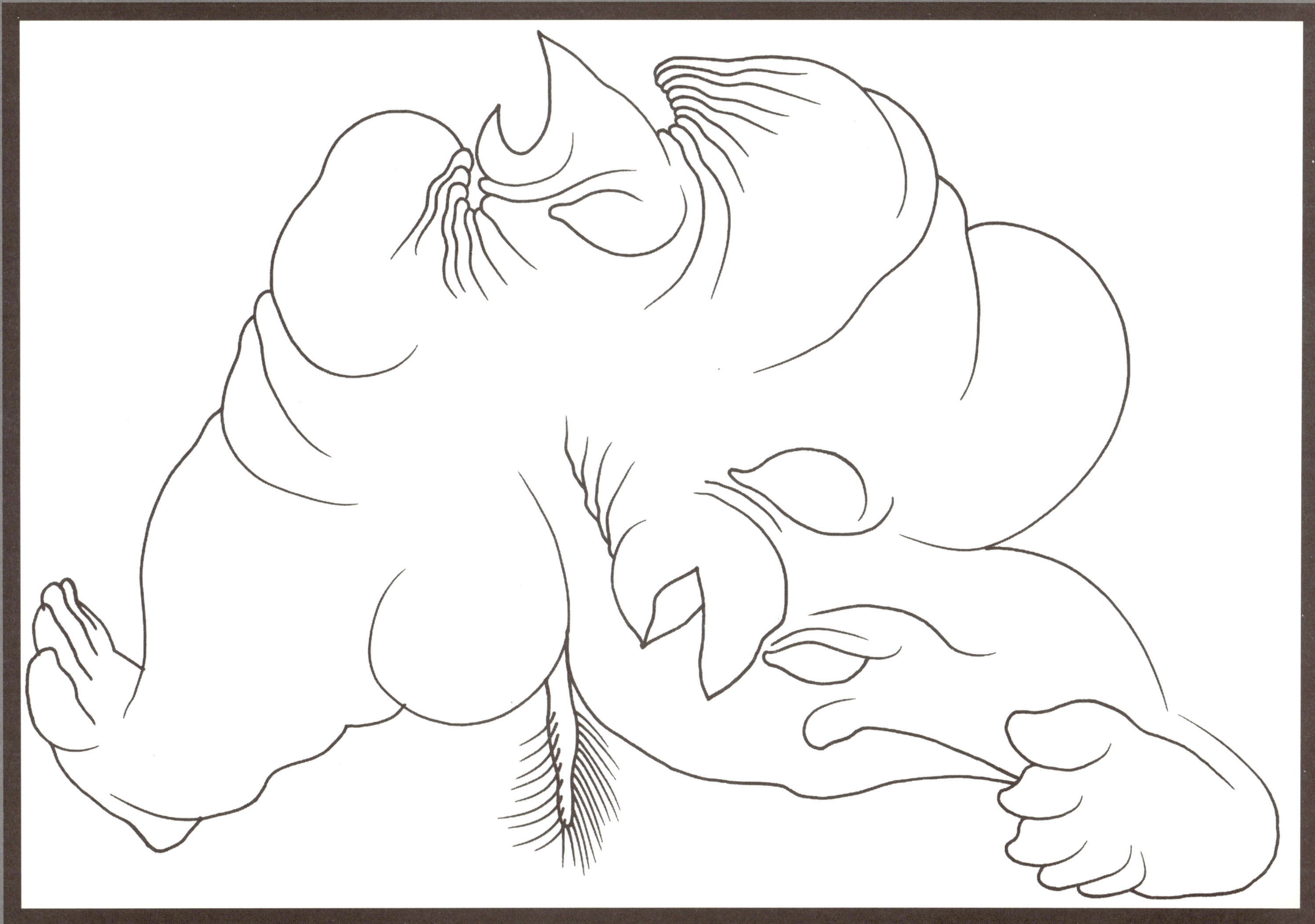

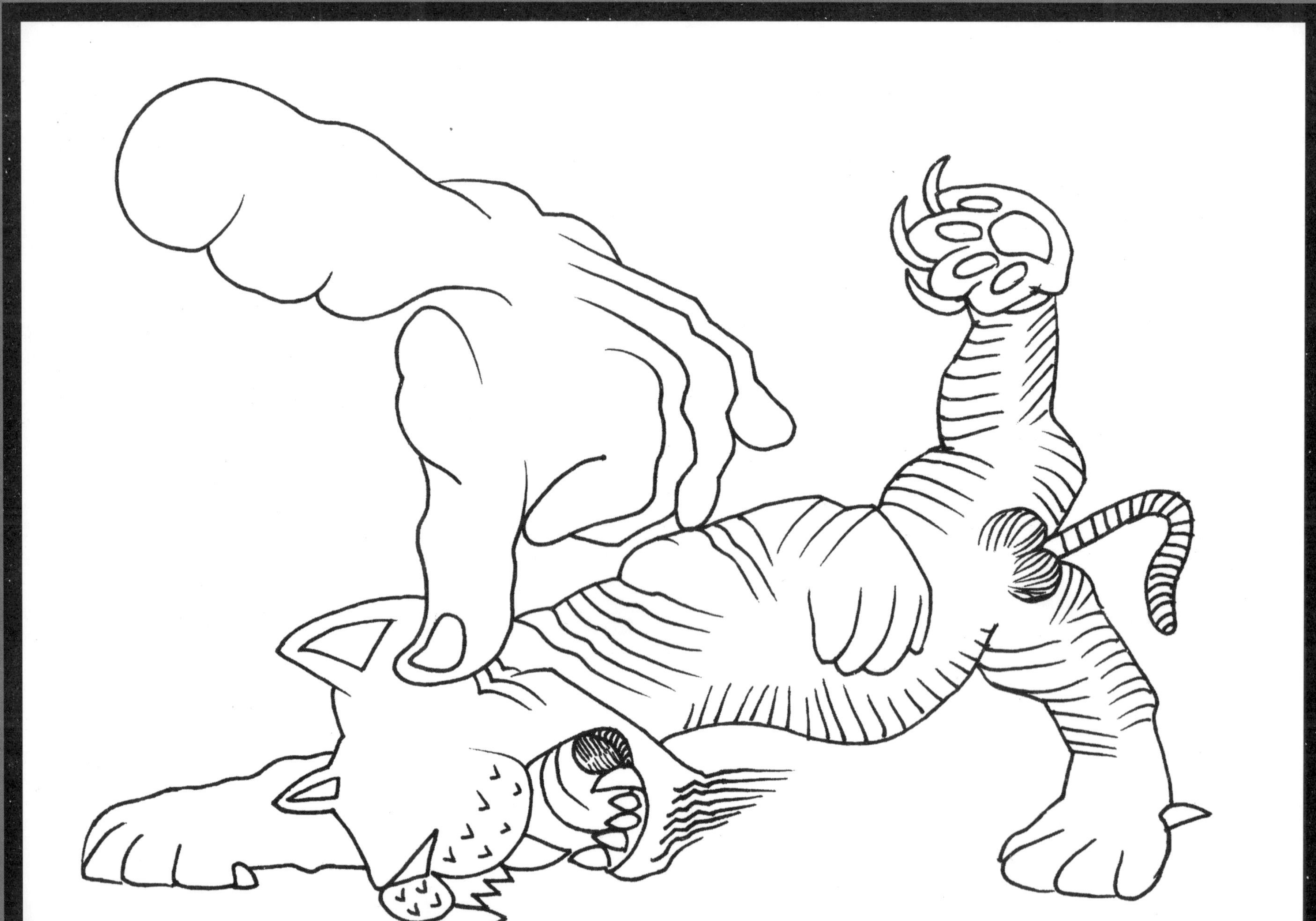

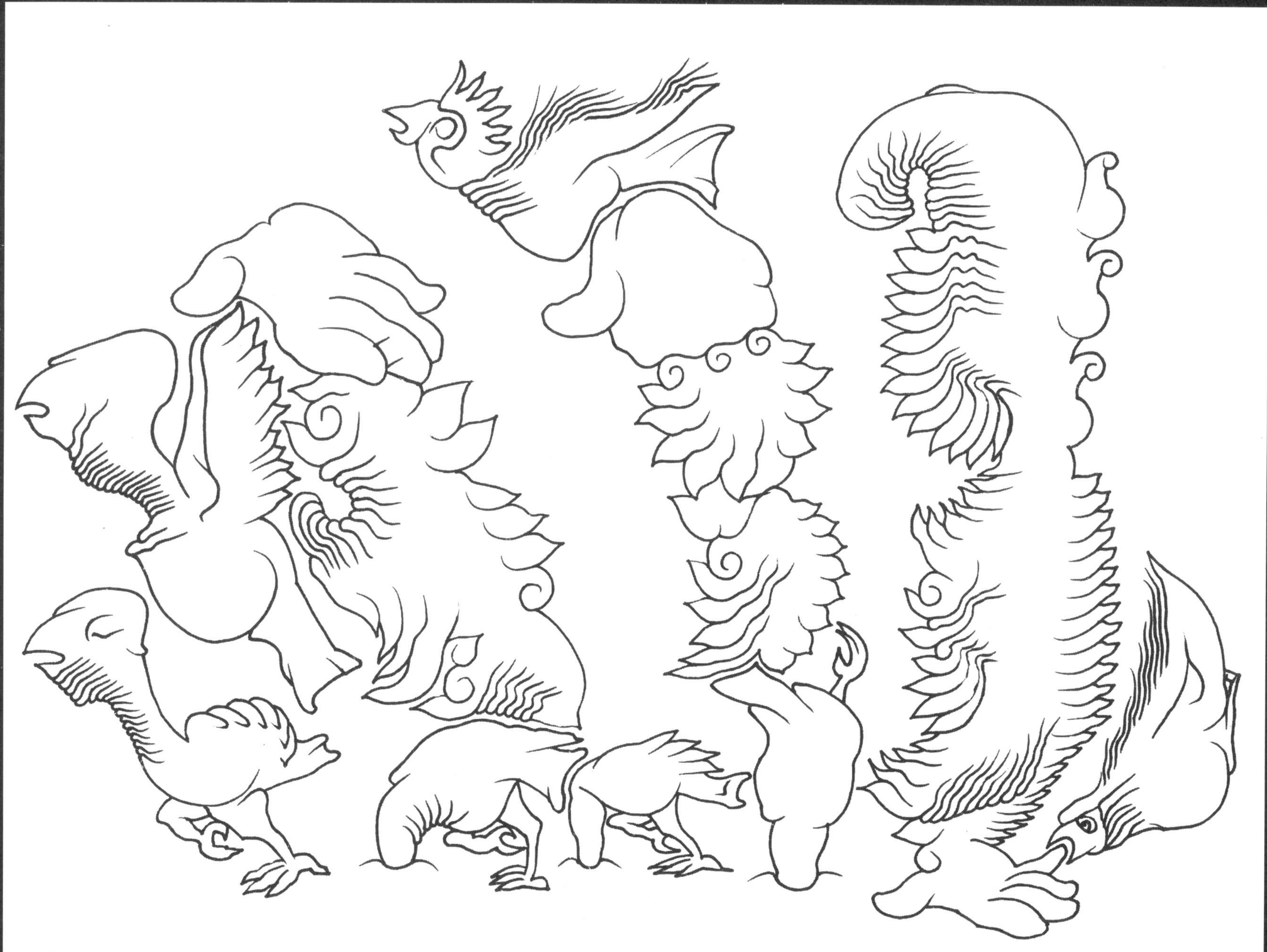

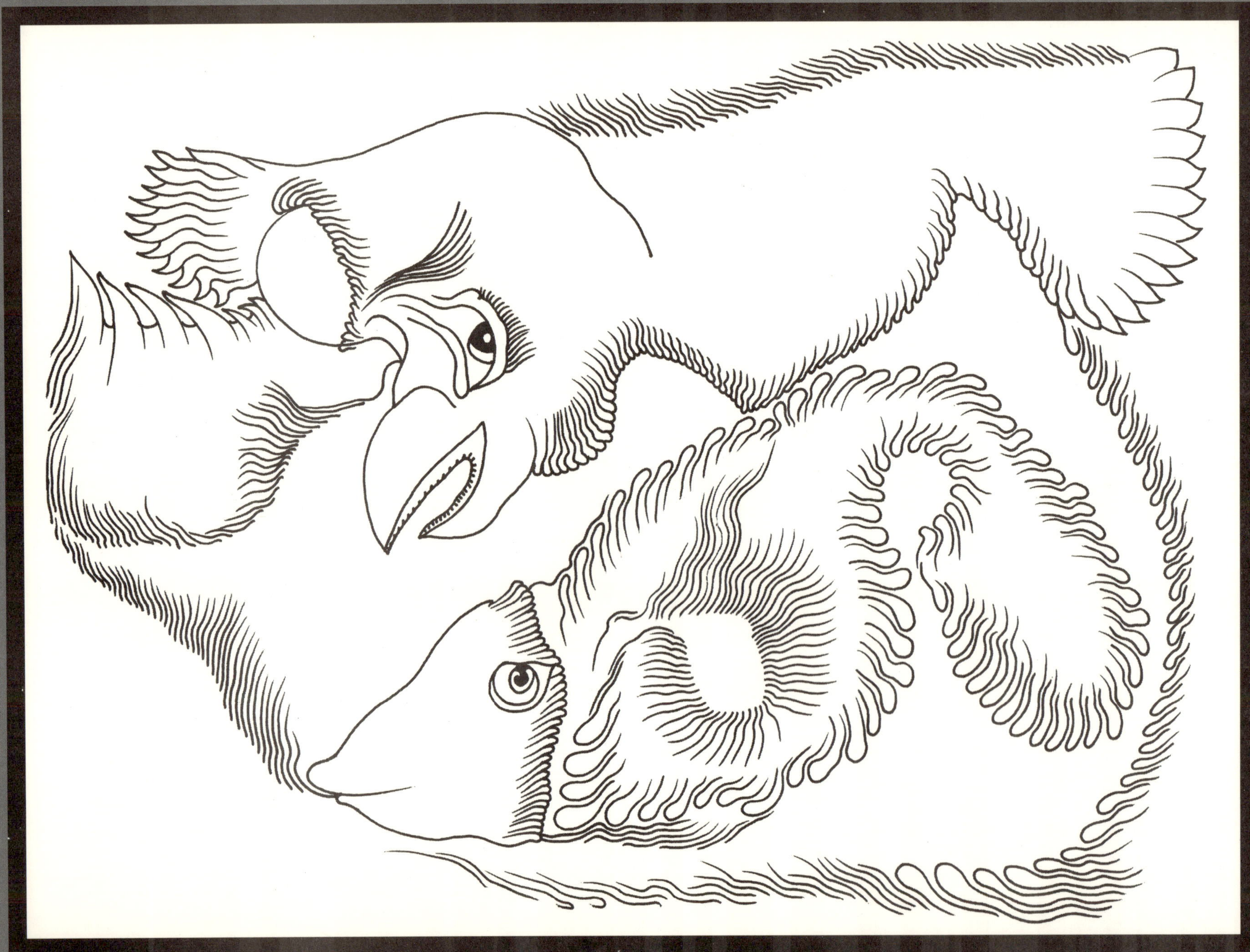

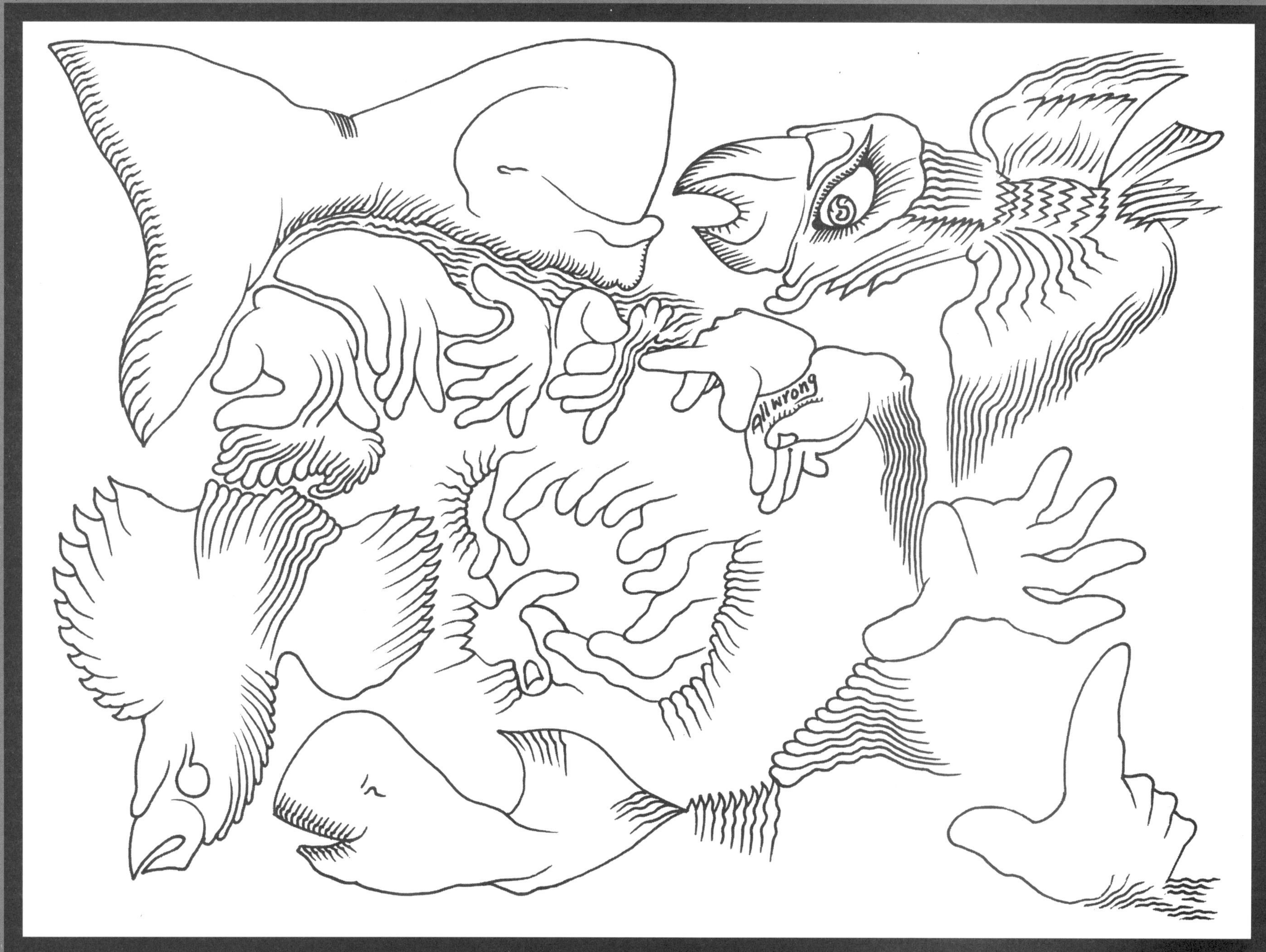
All wrong

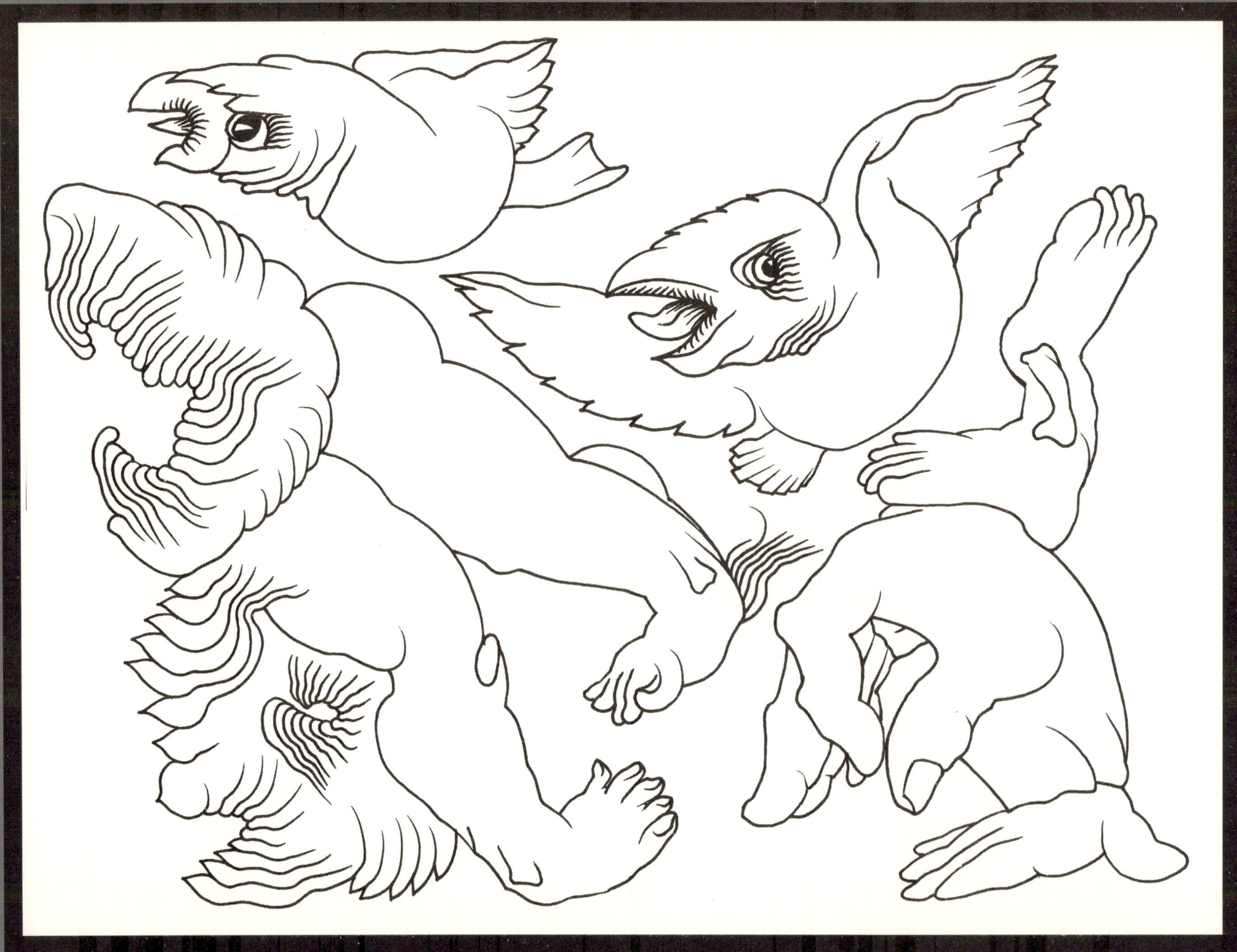

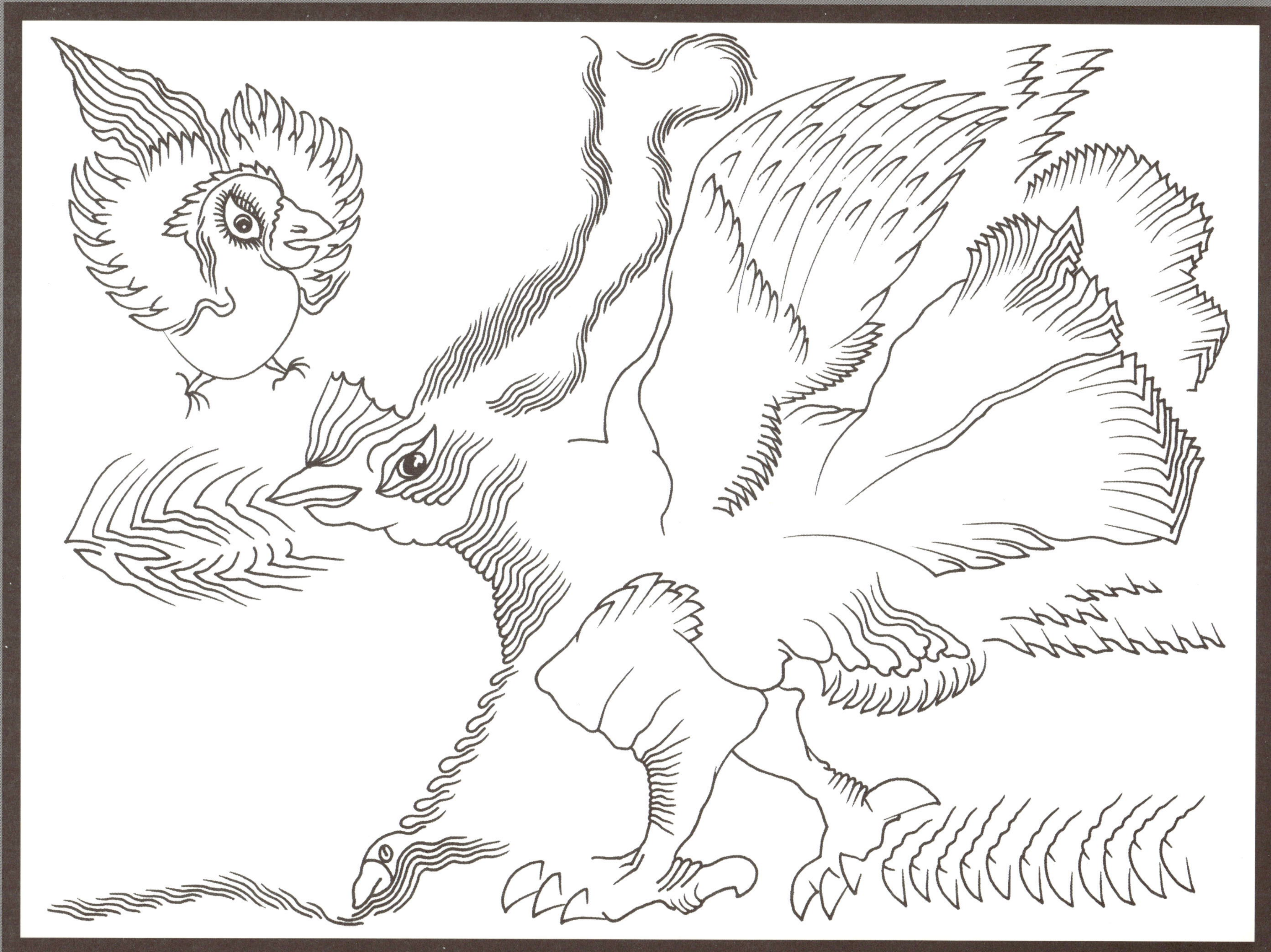

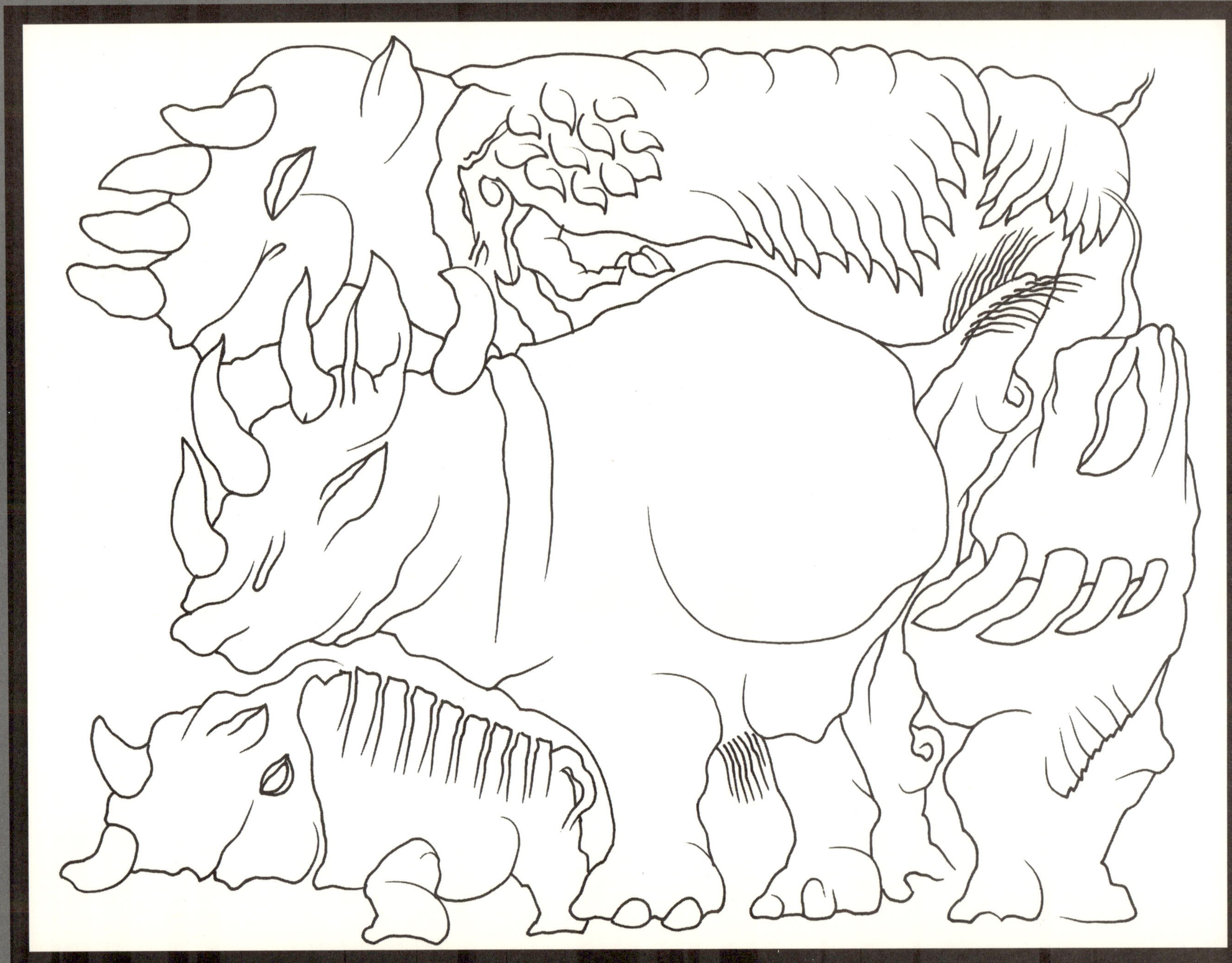

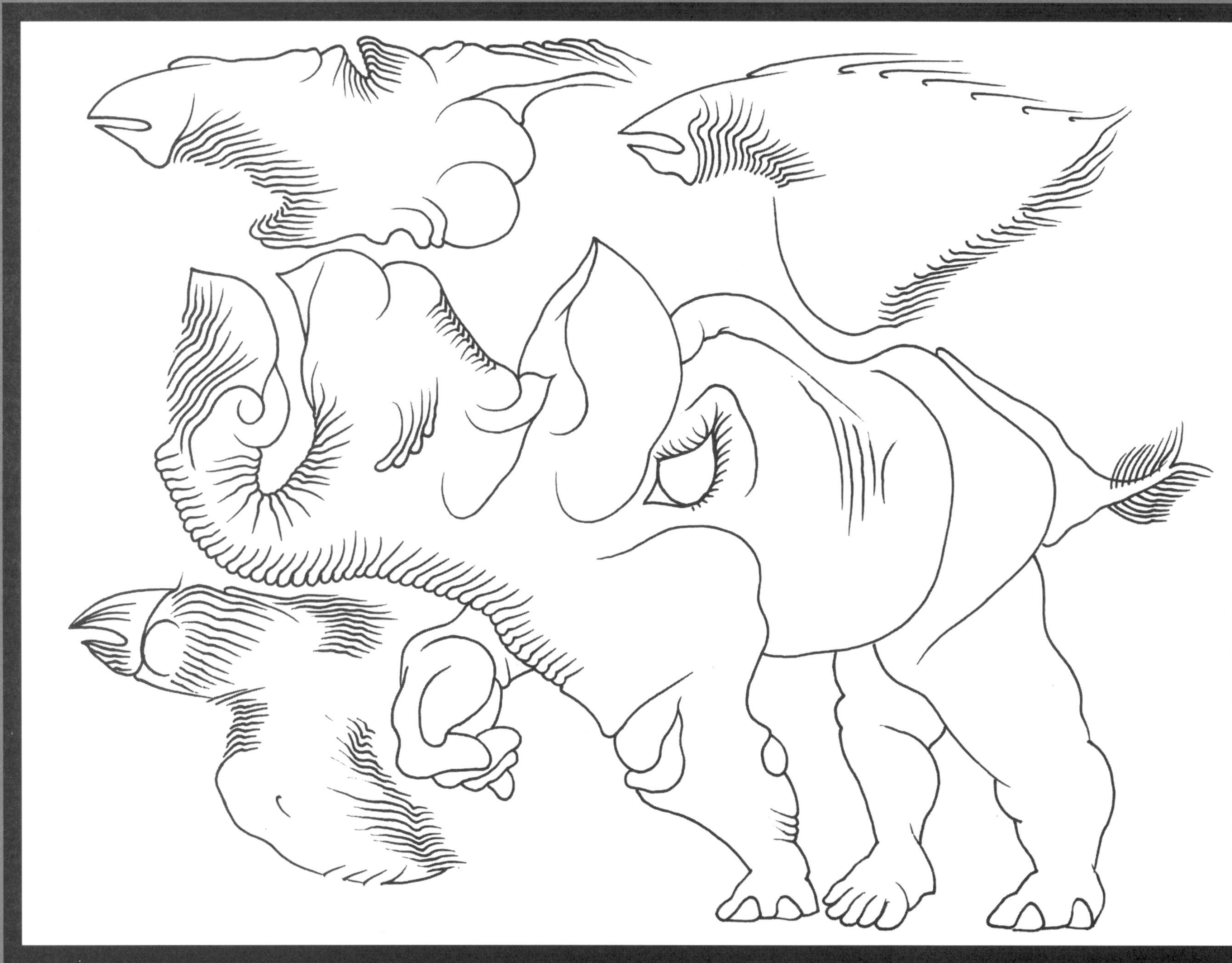

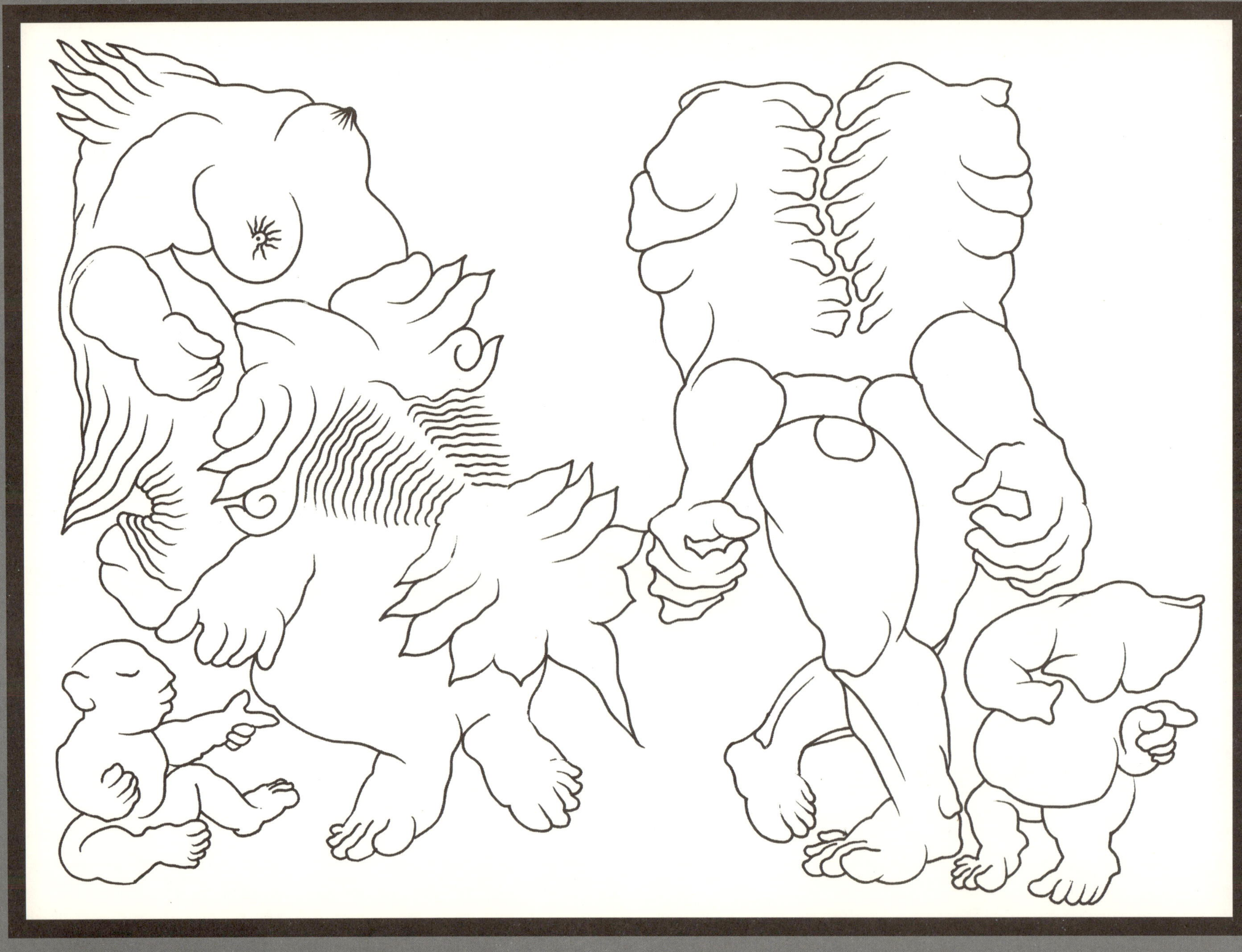

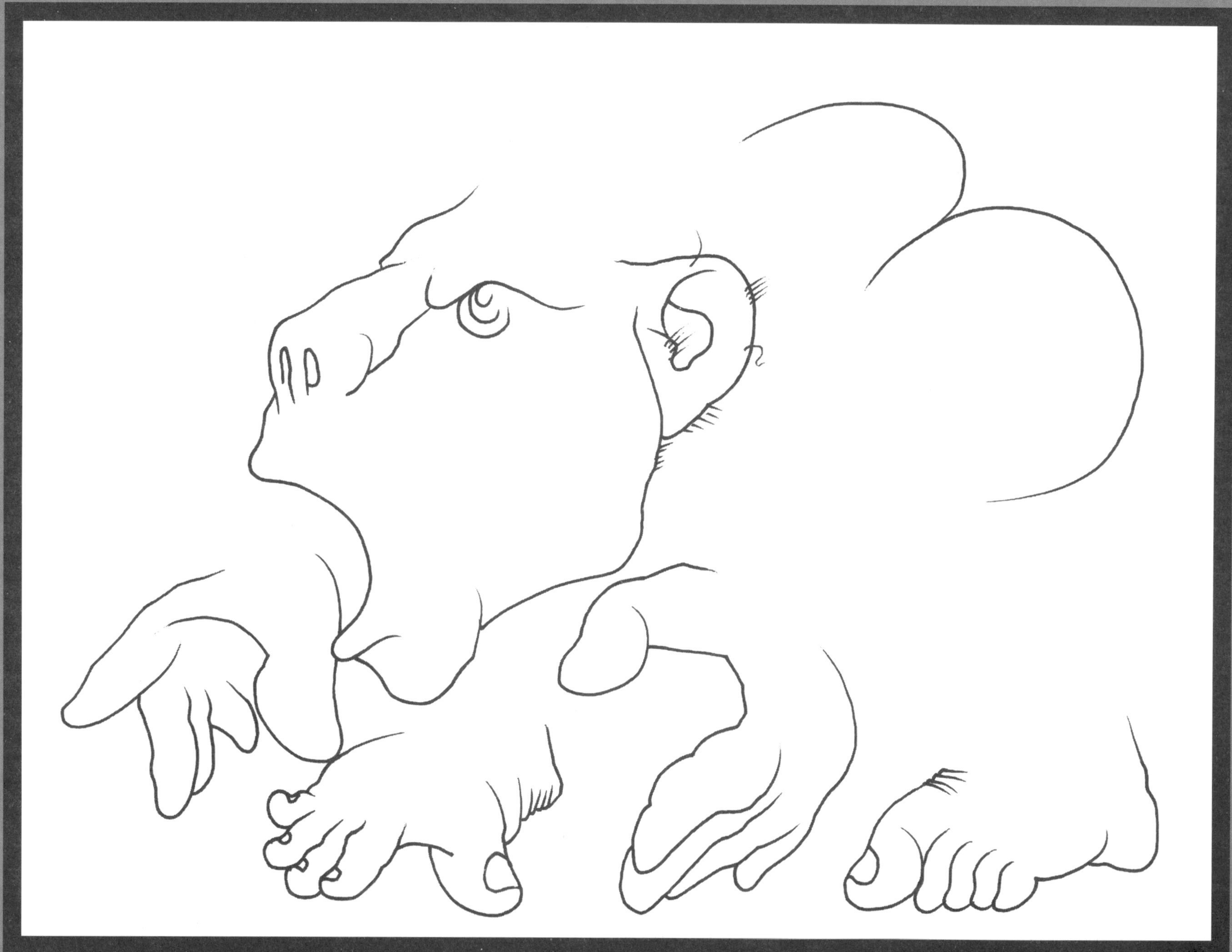

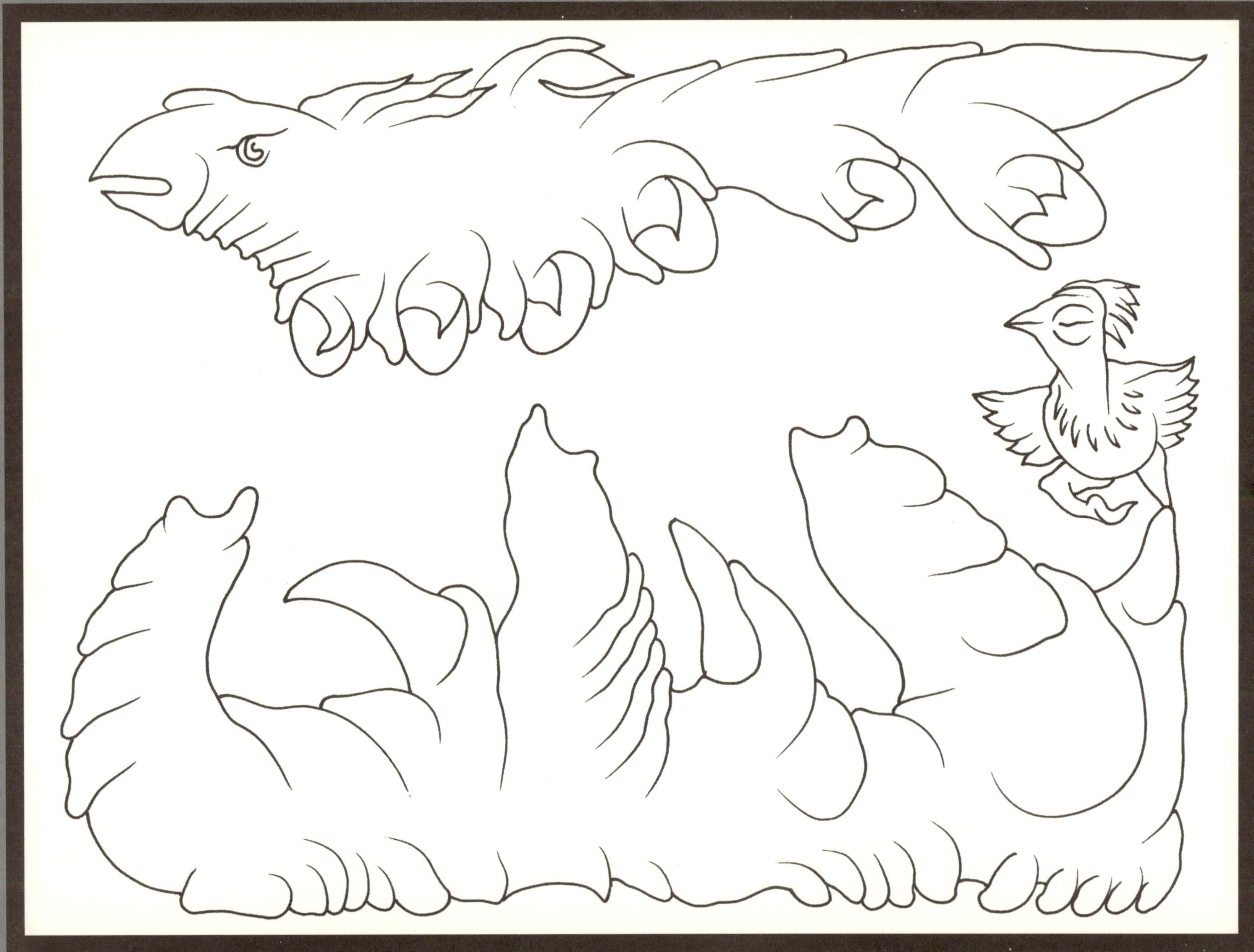

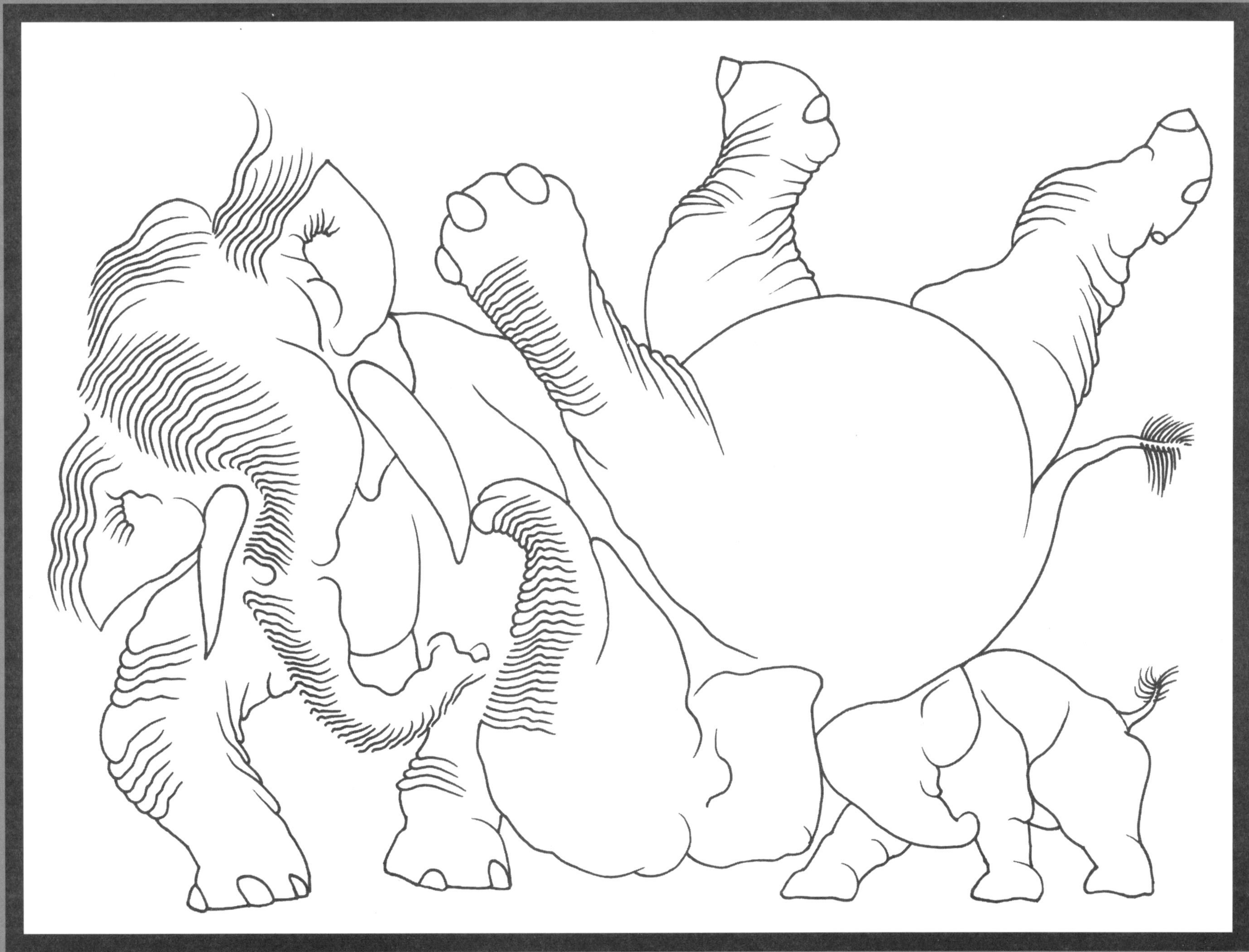

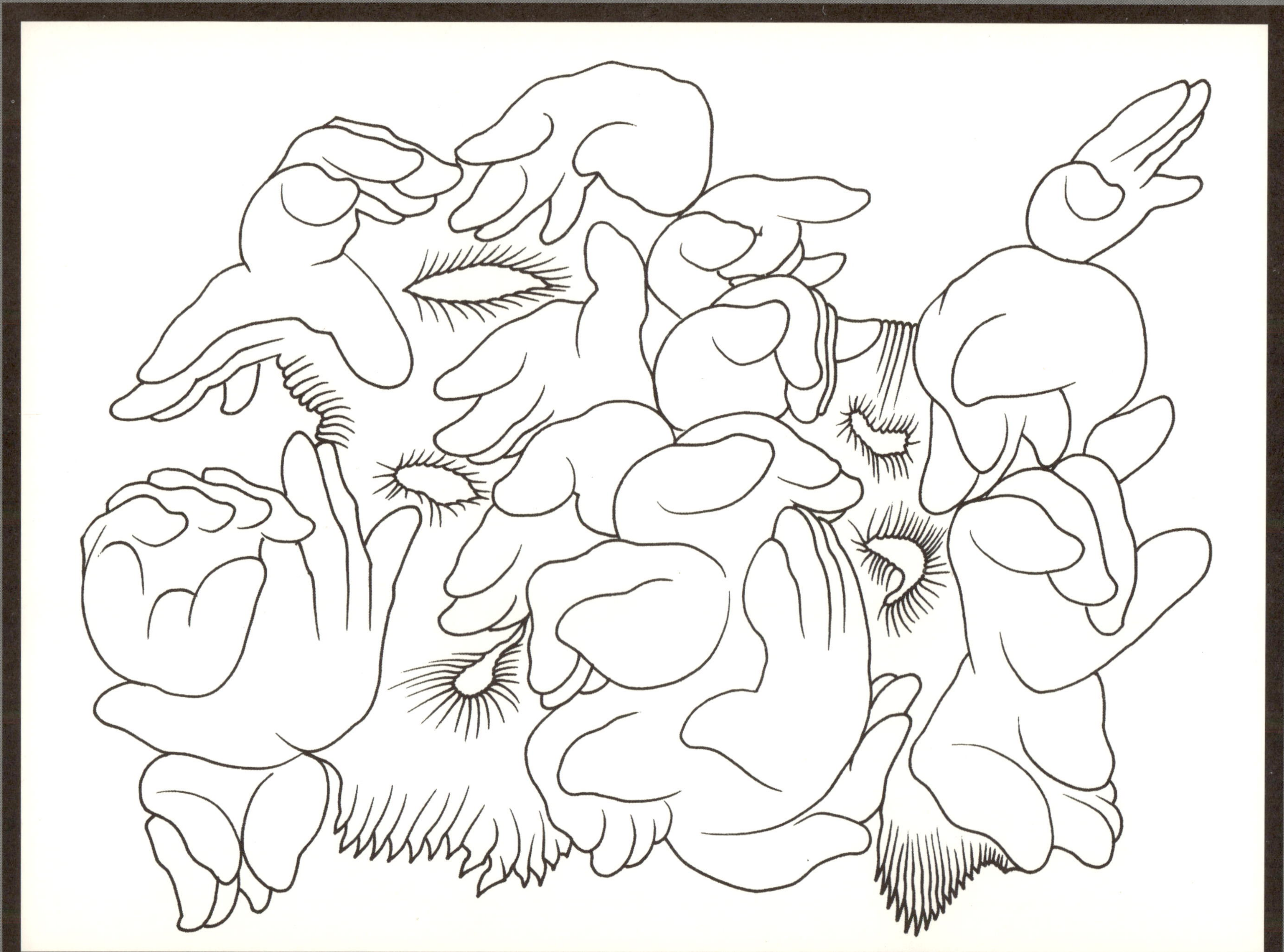

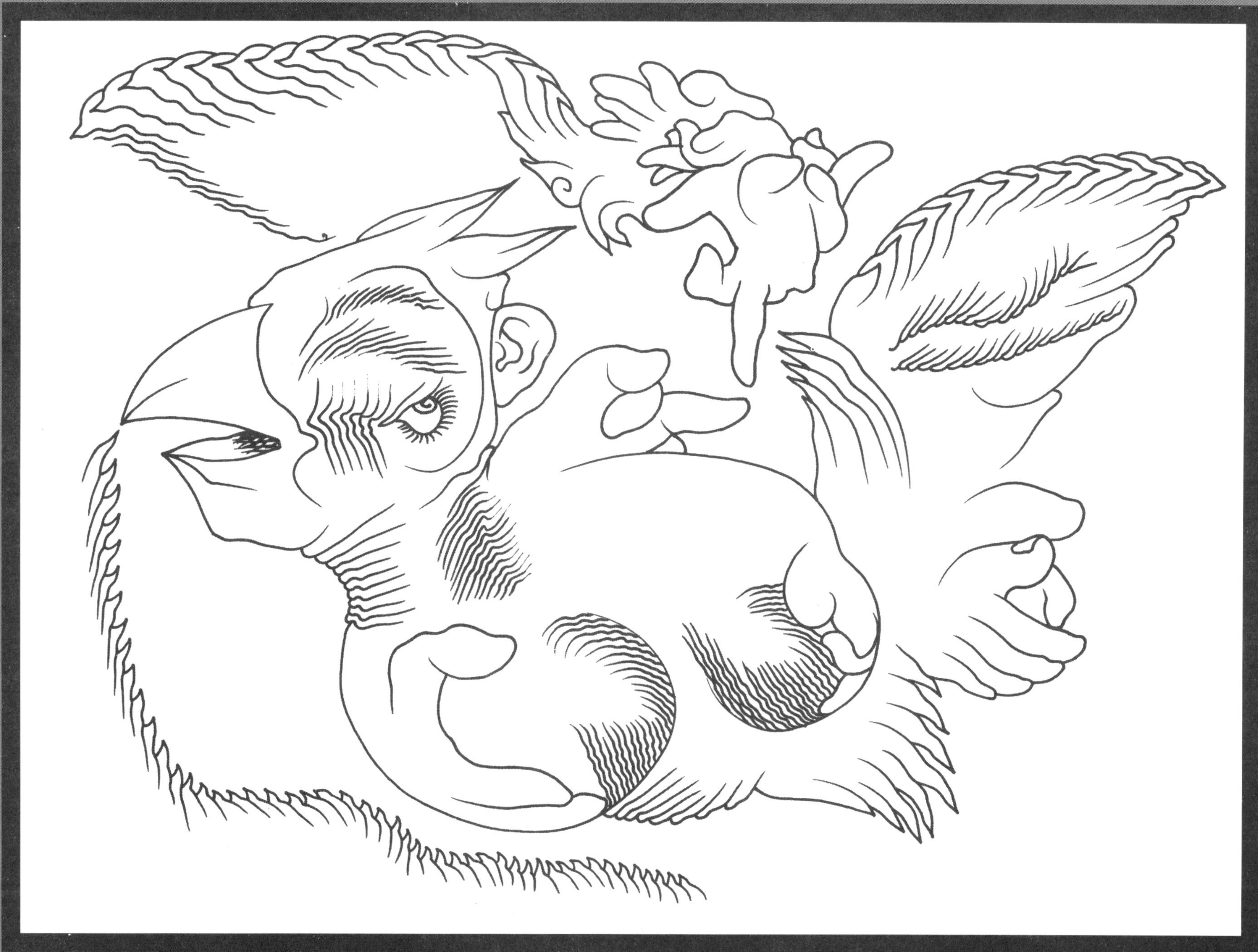

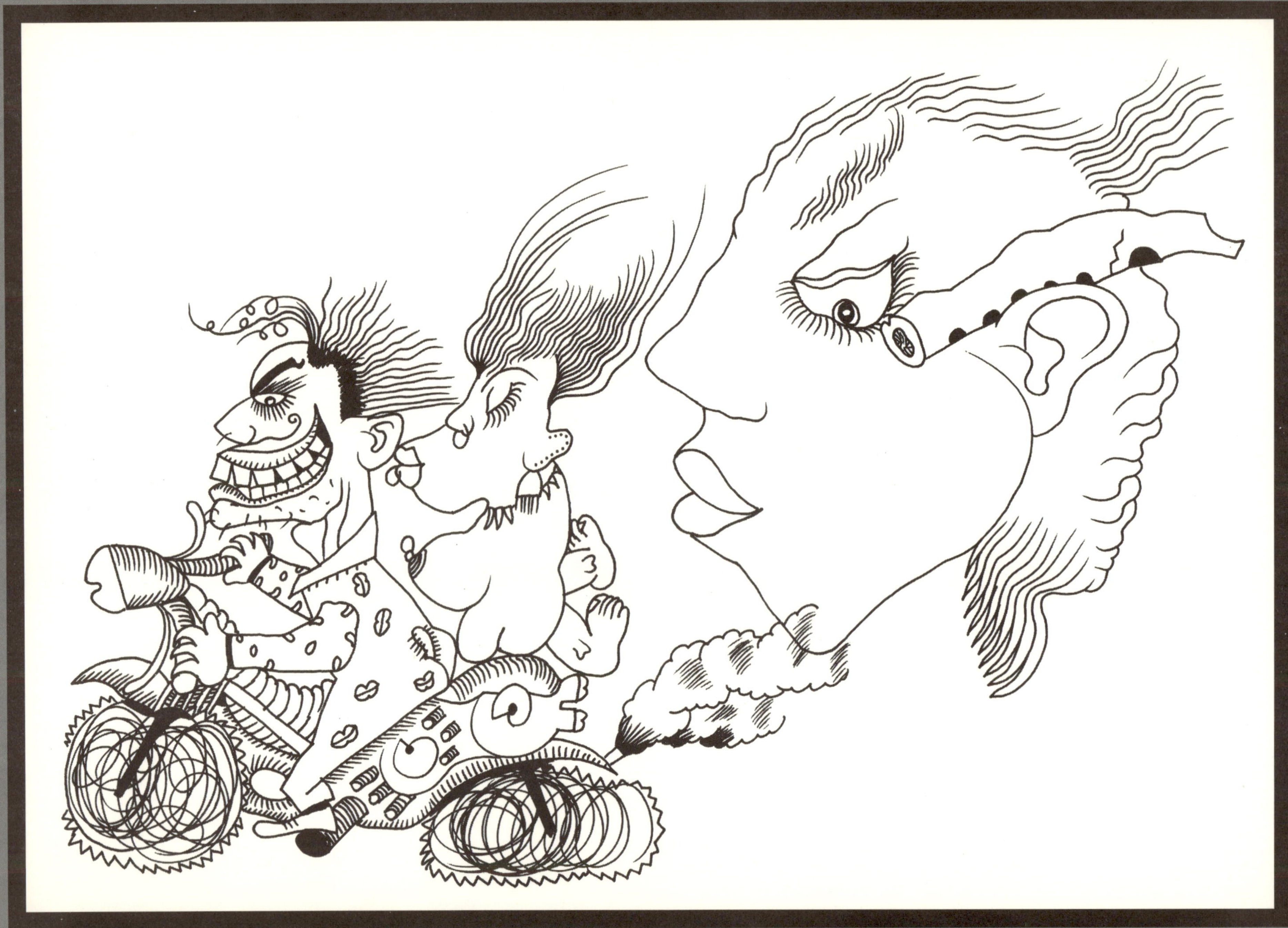

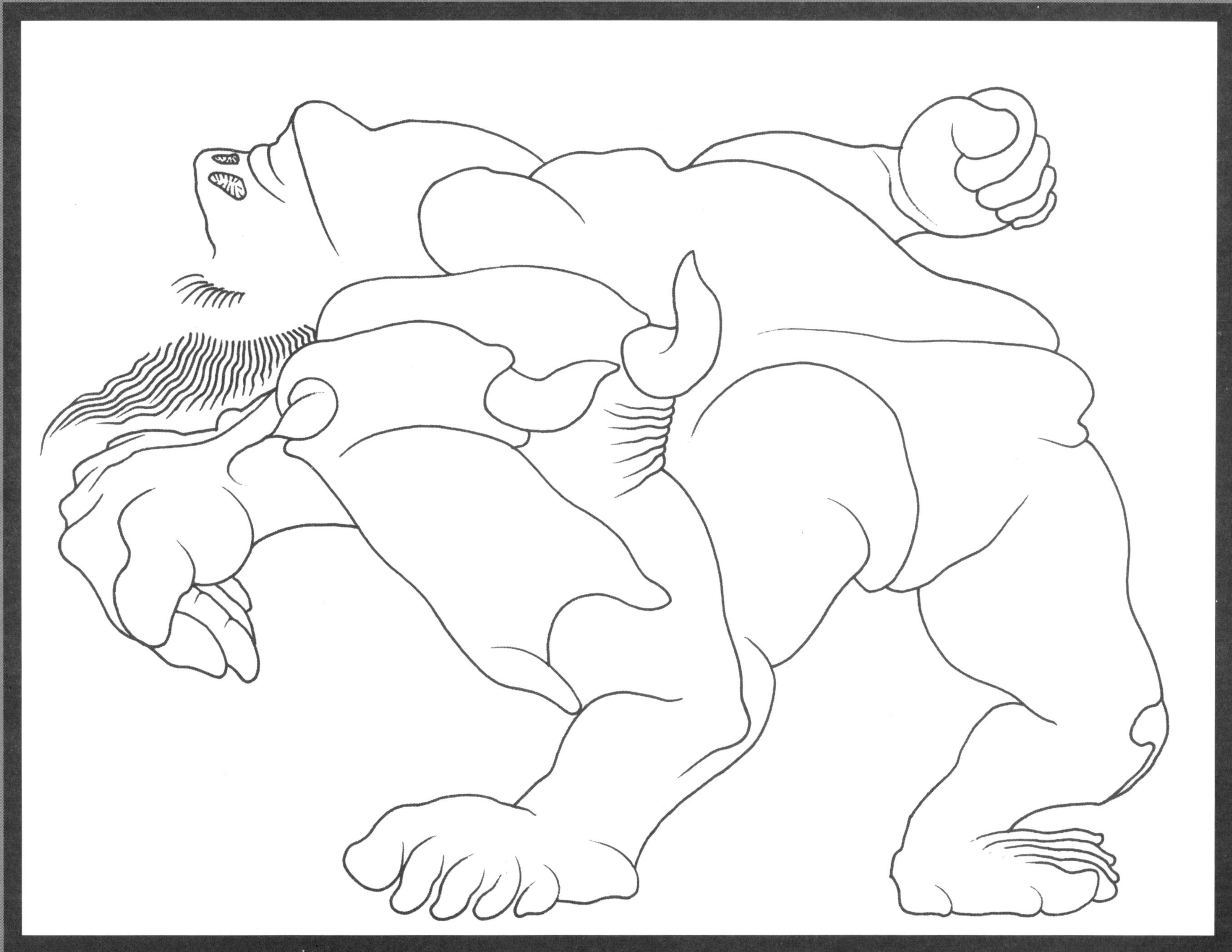

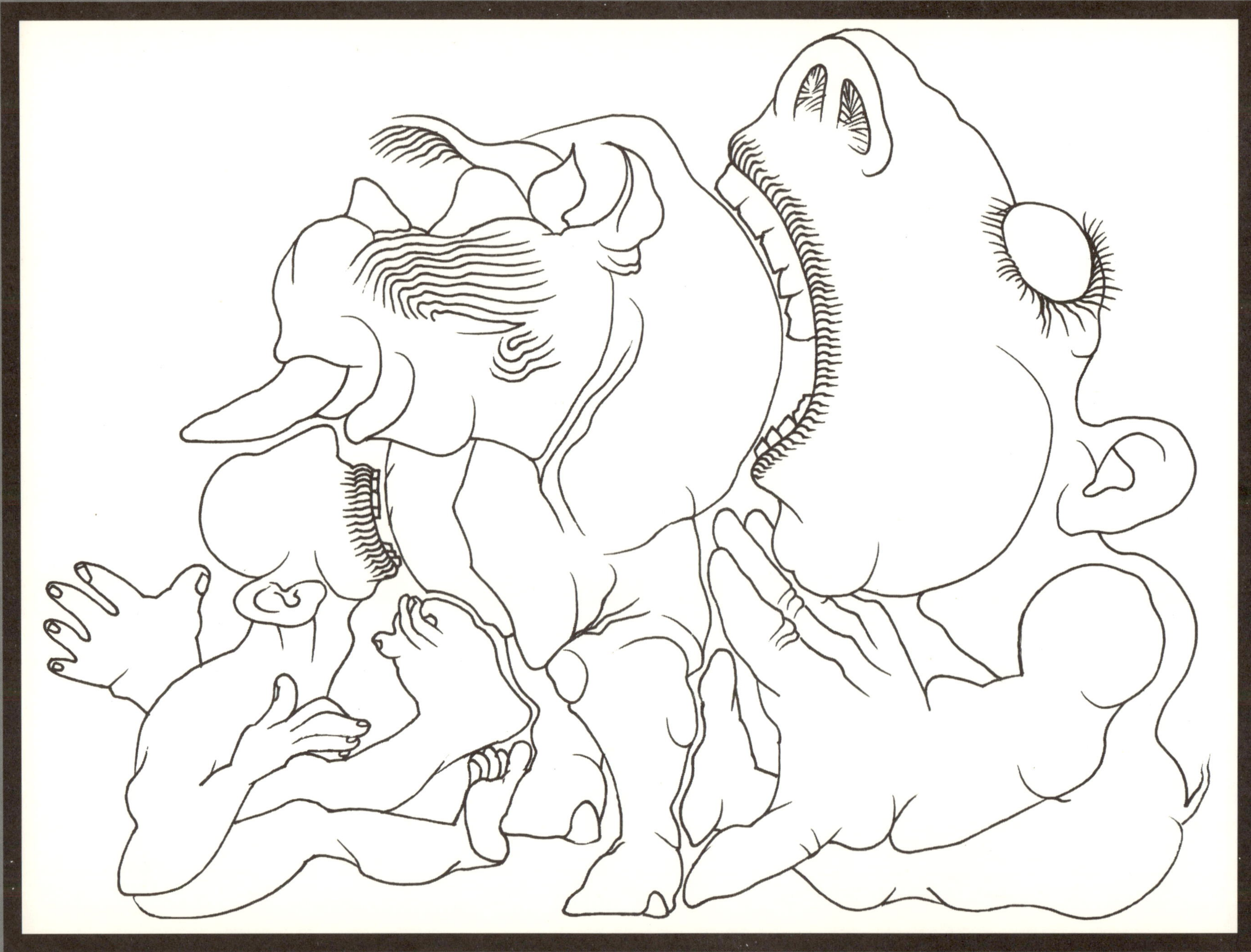

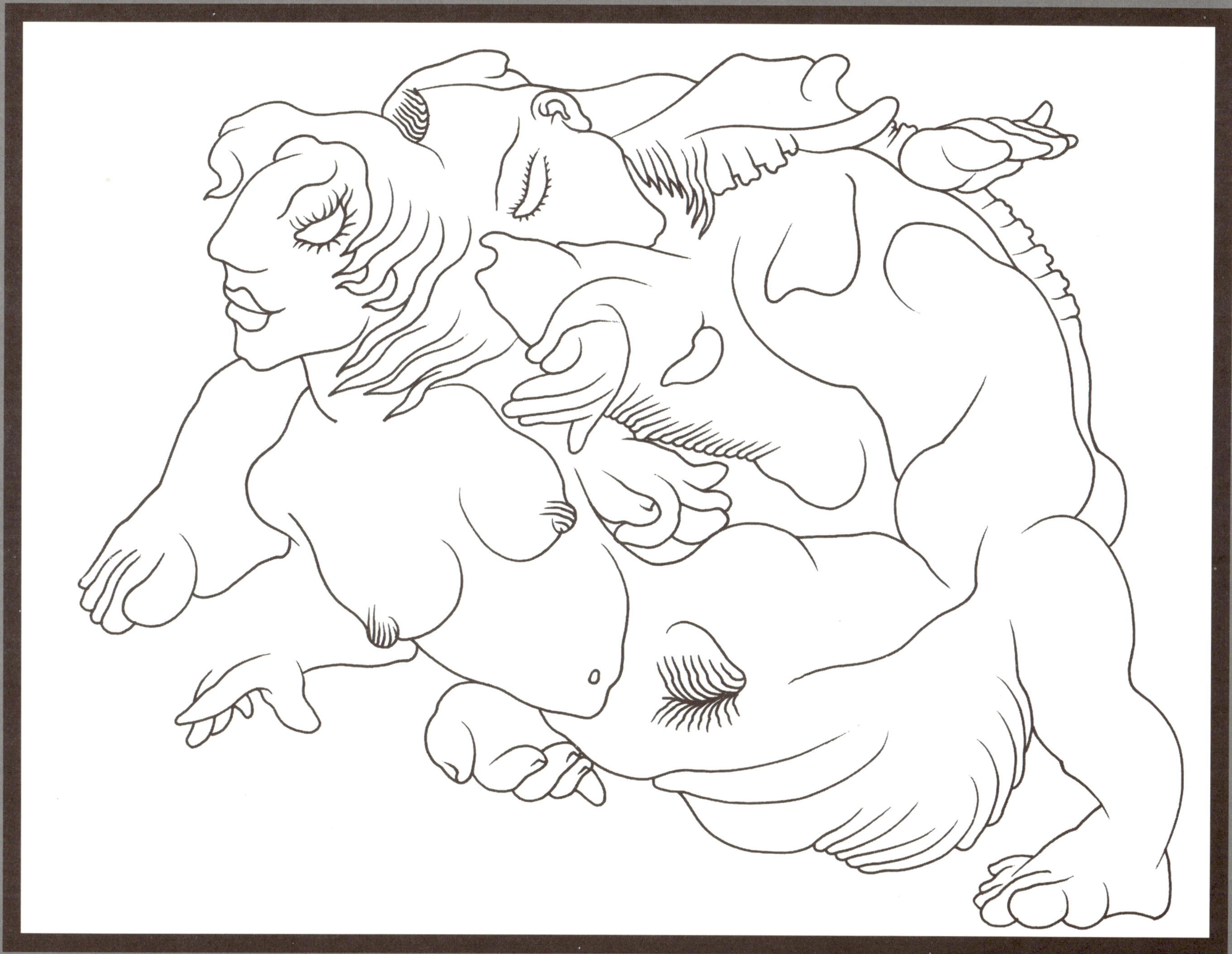

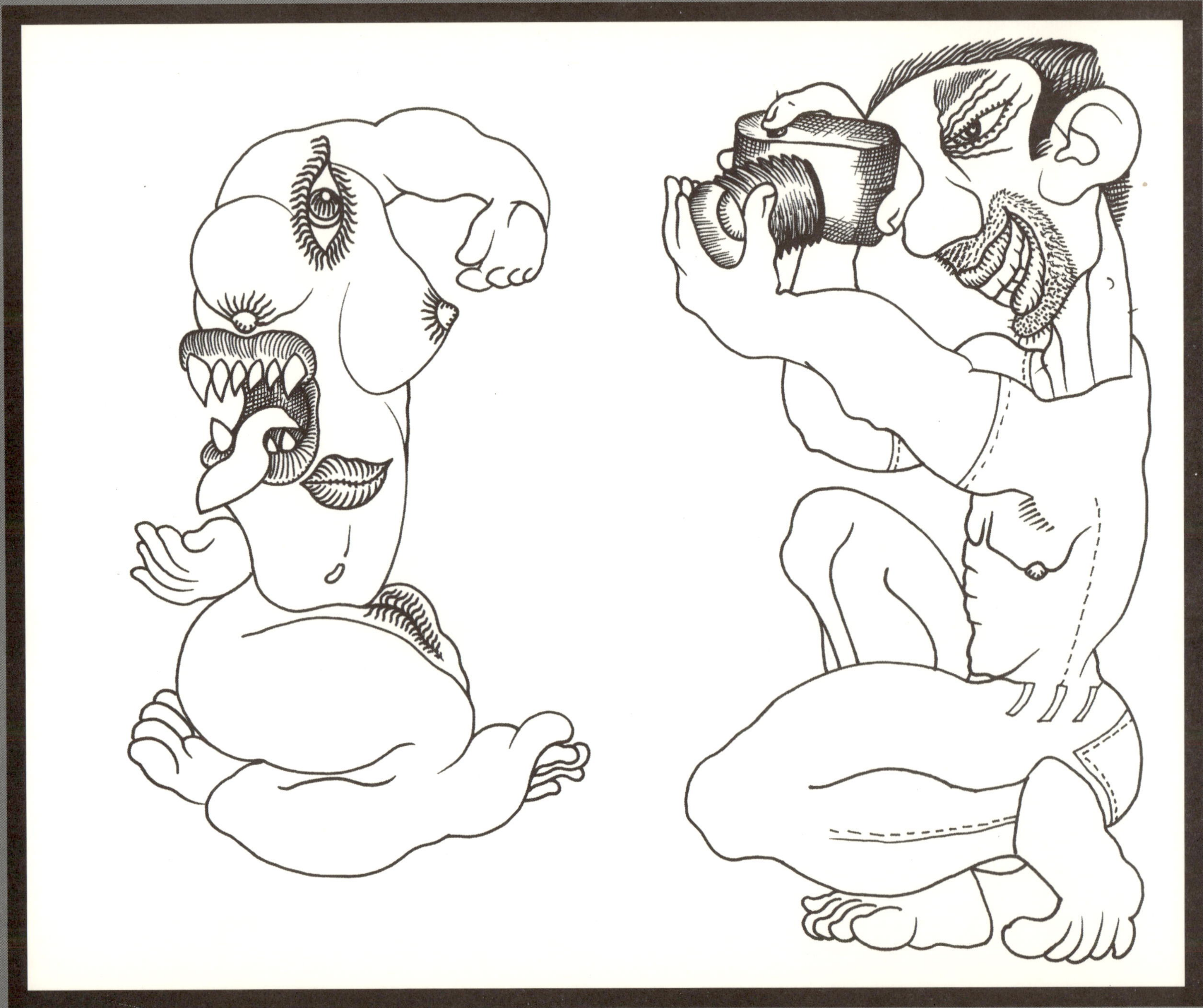

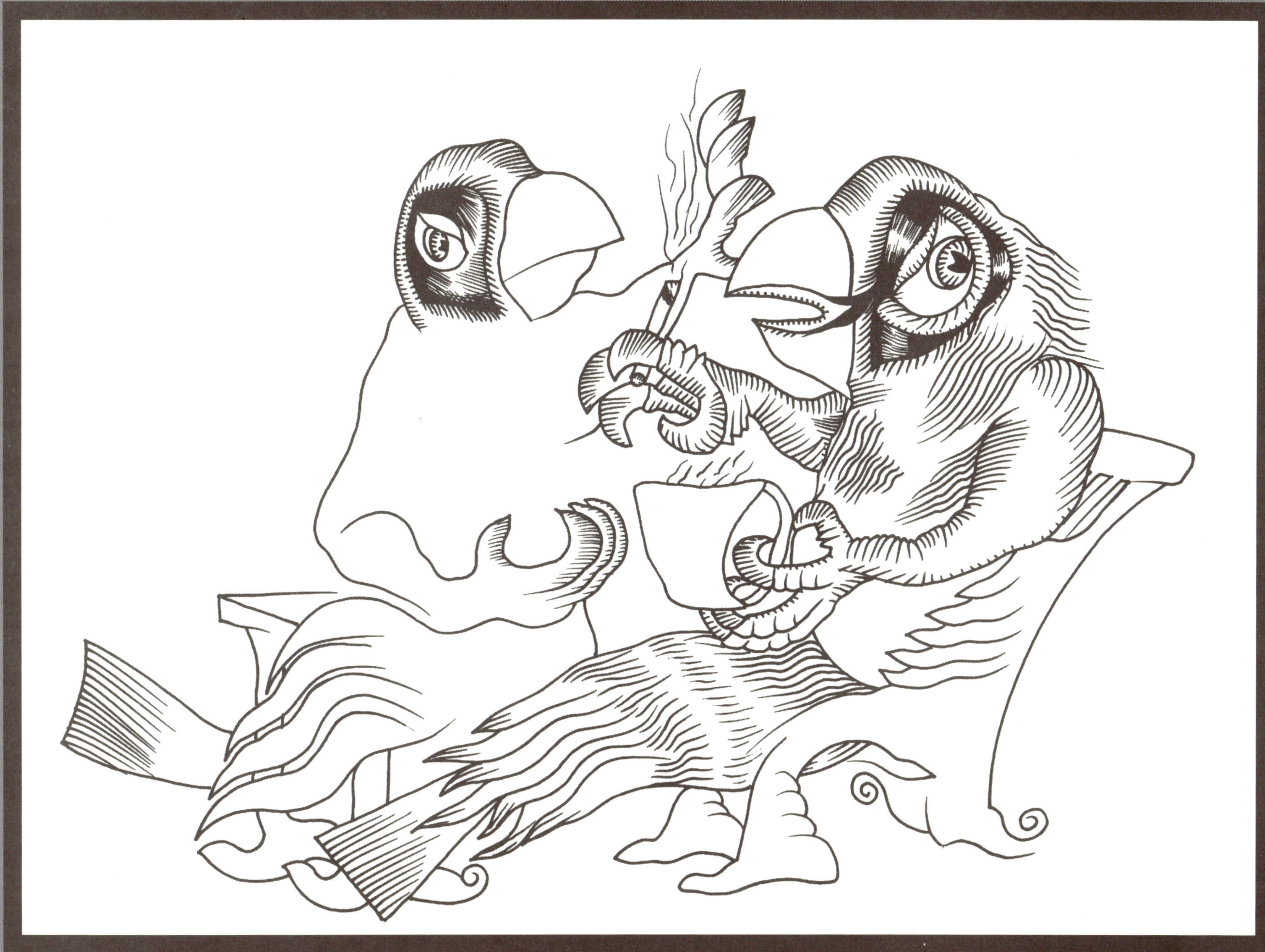

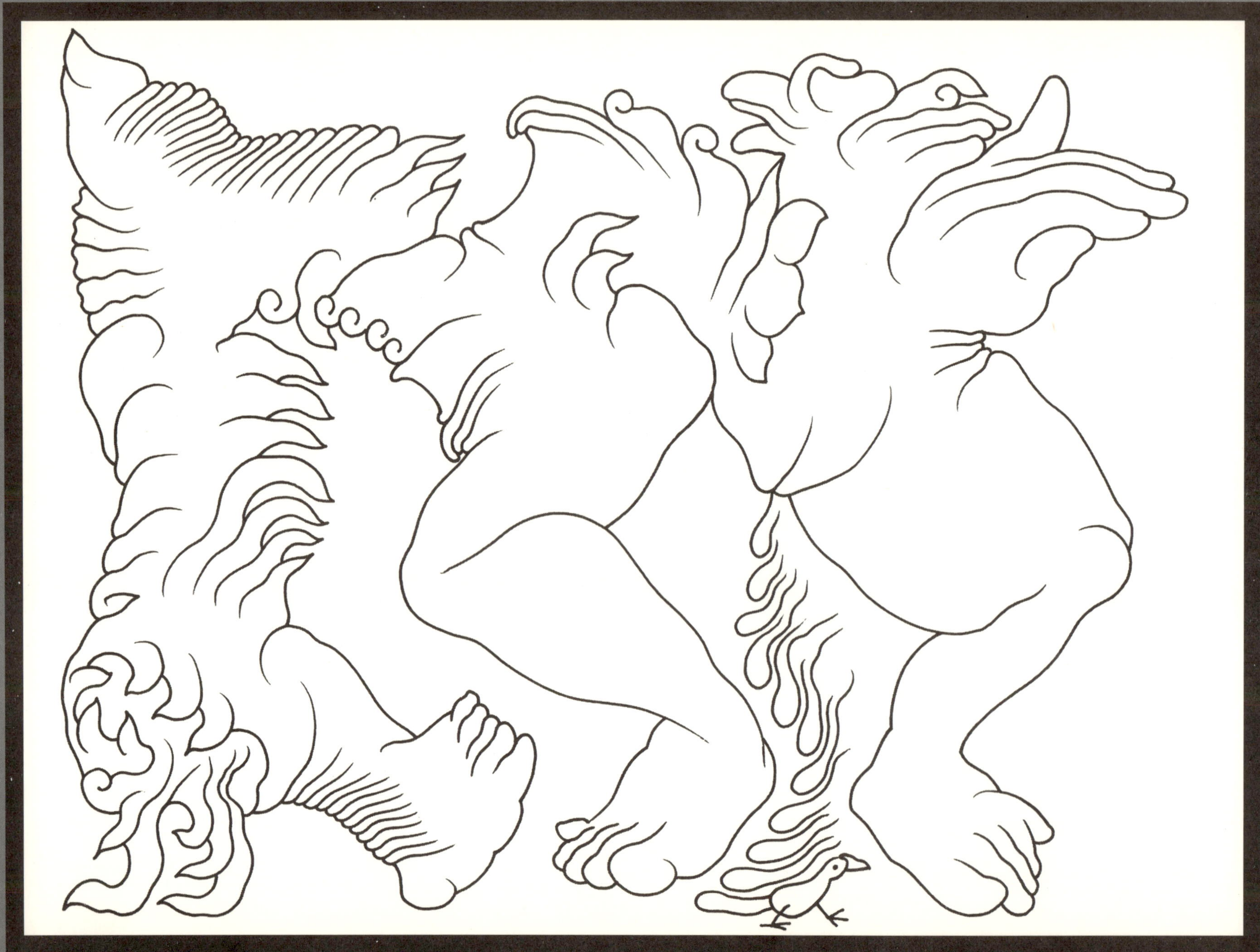

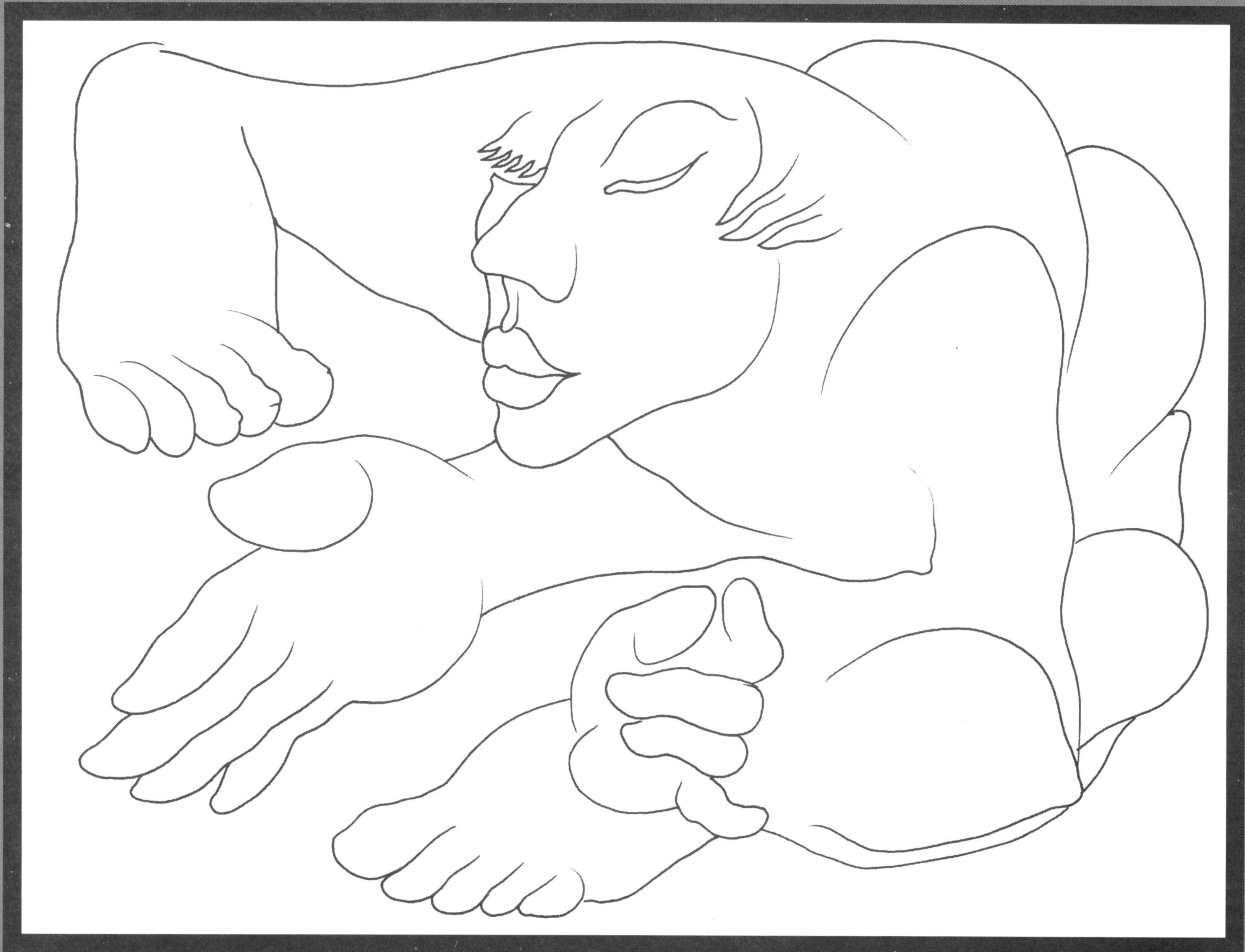

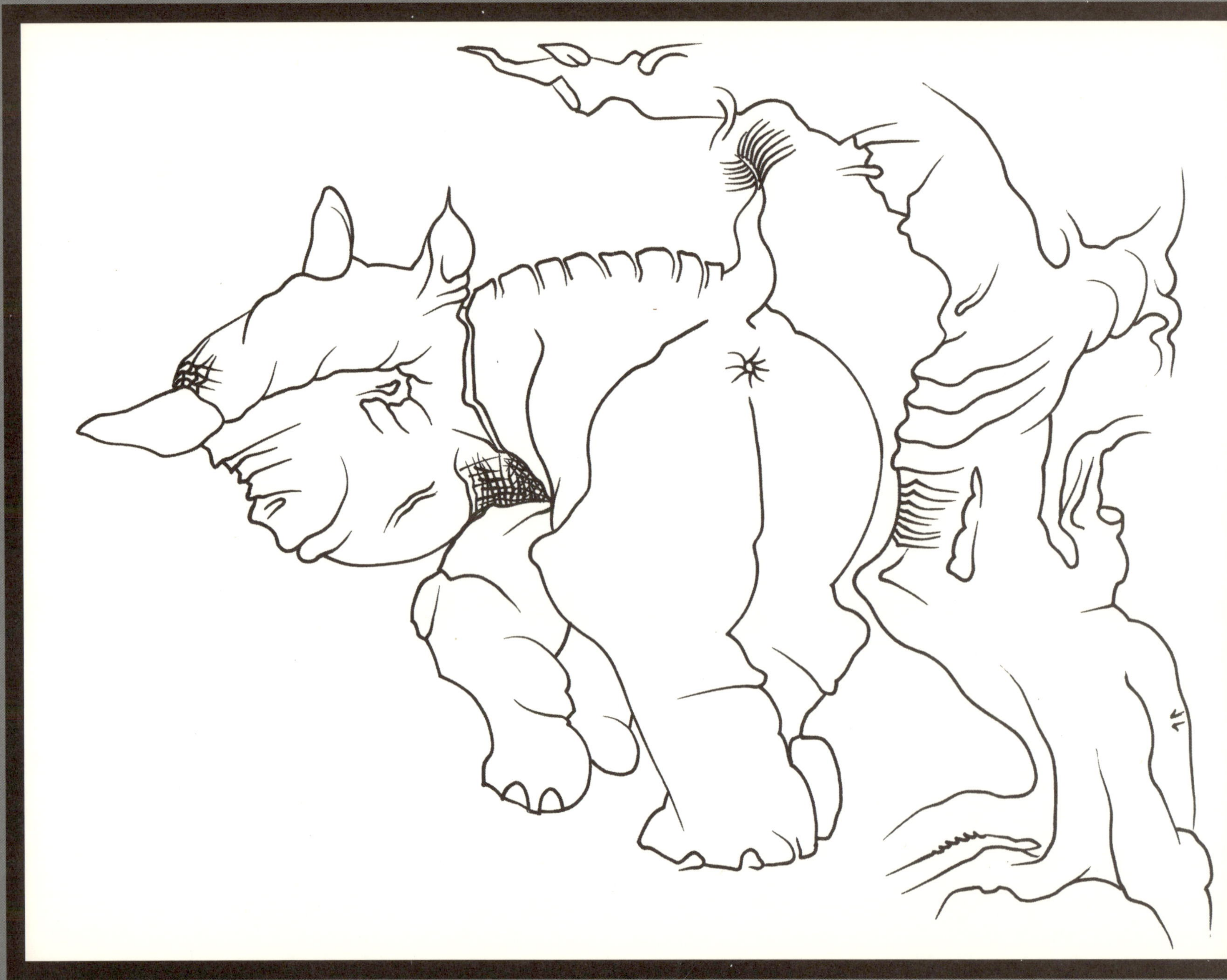

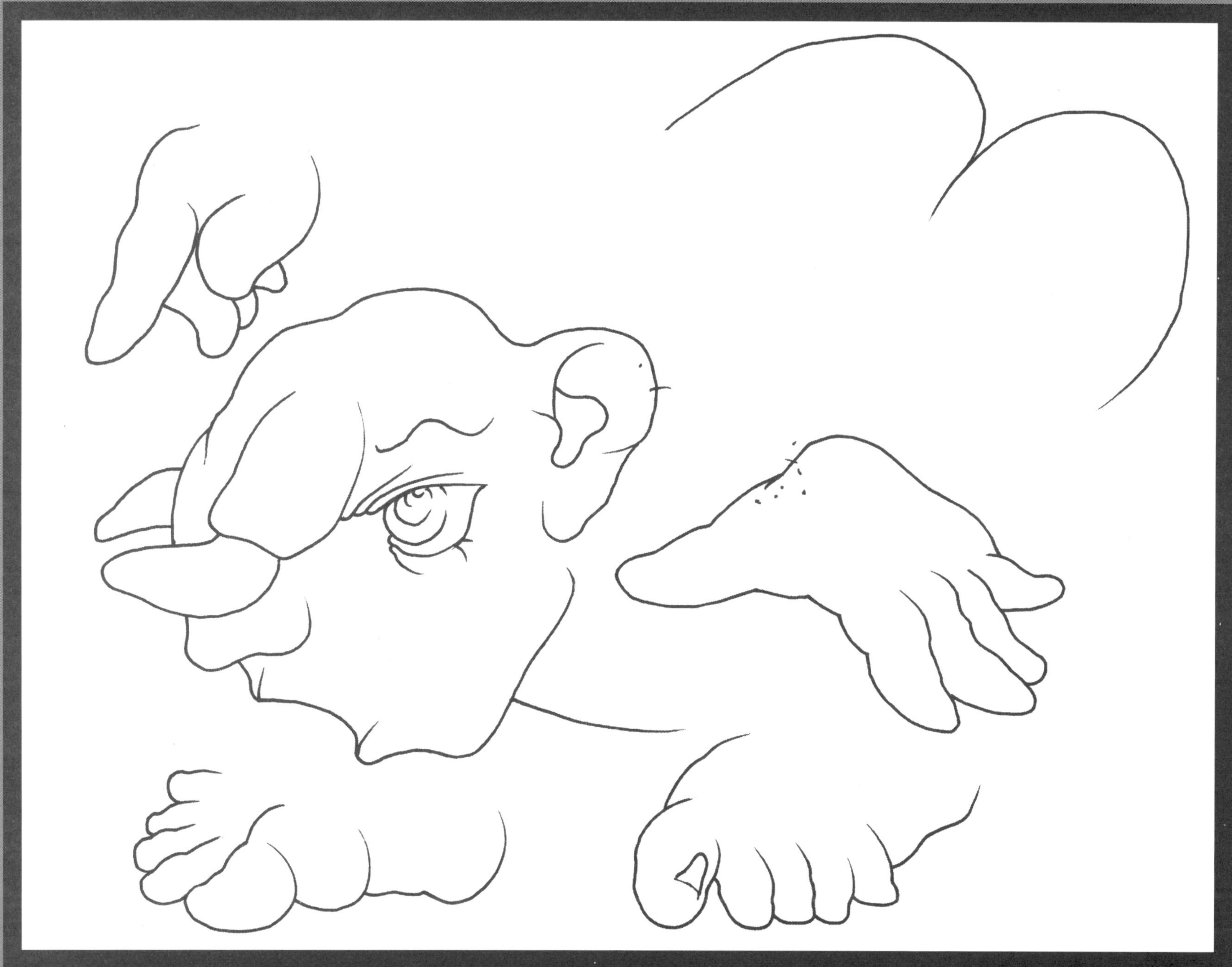

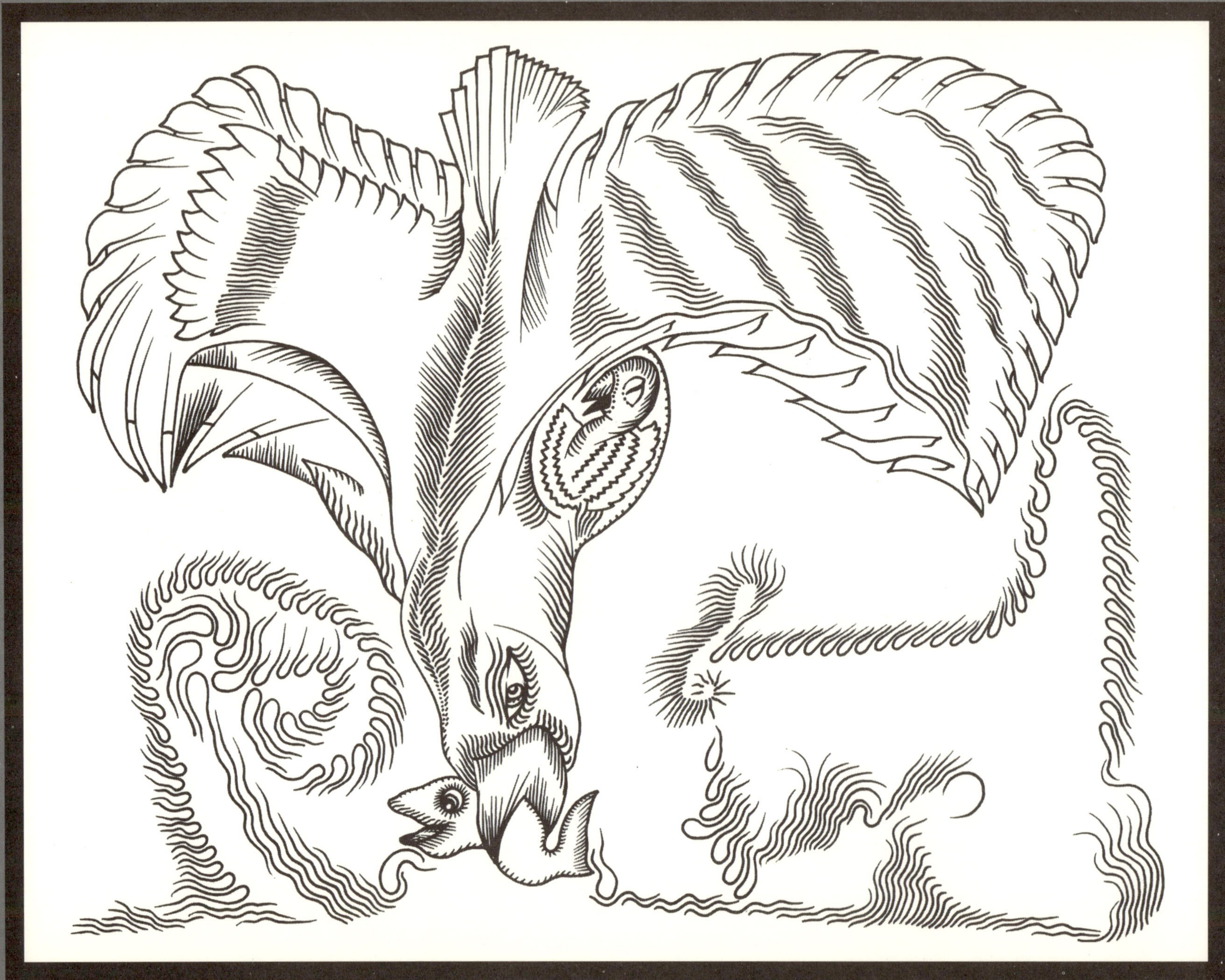

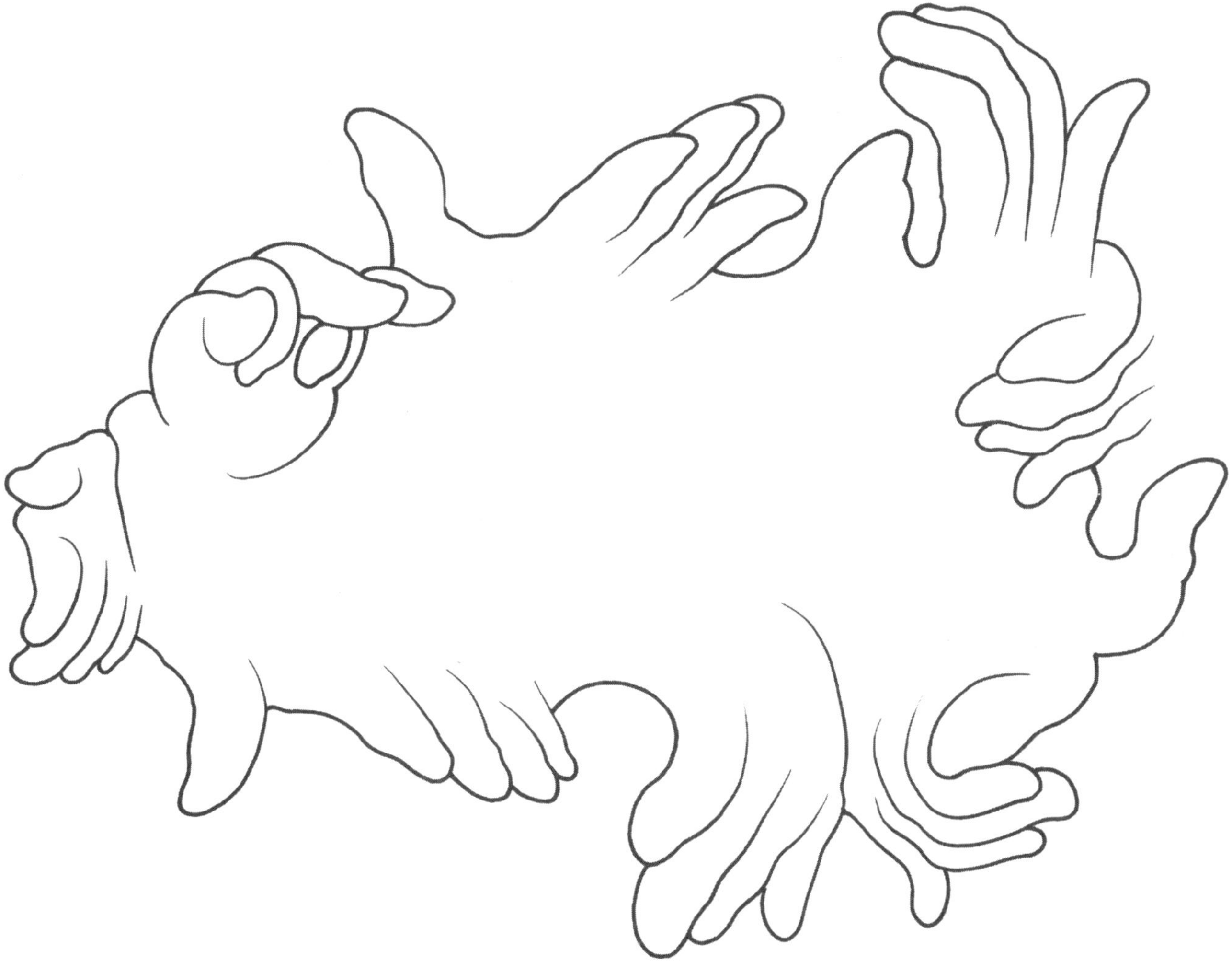

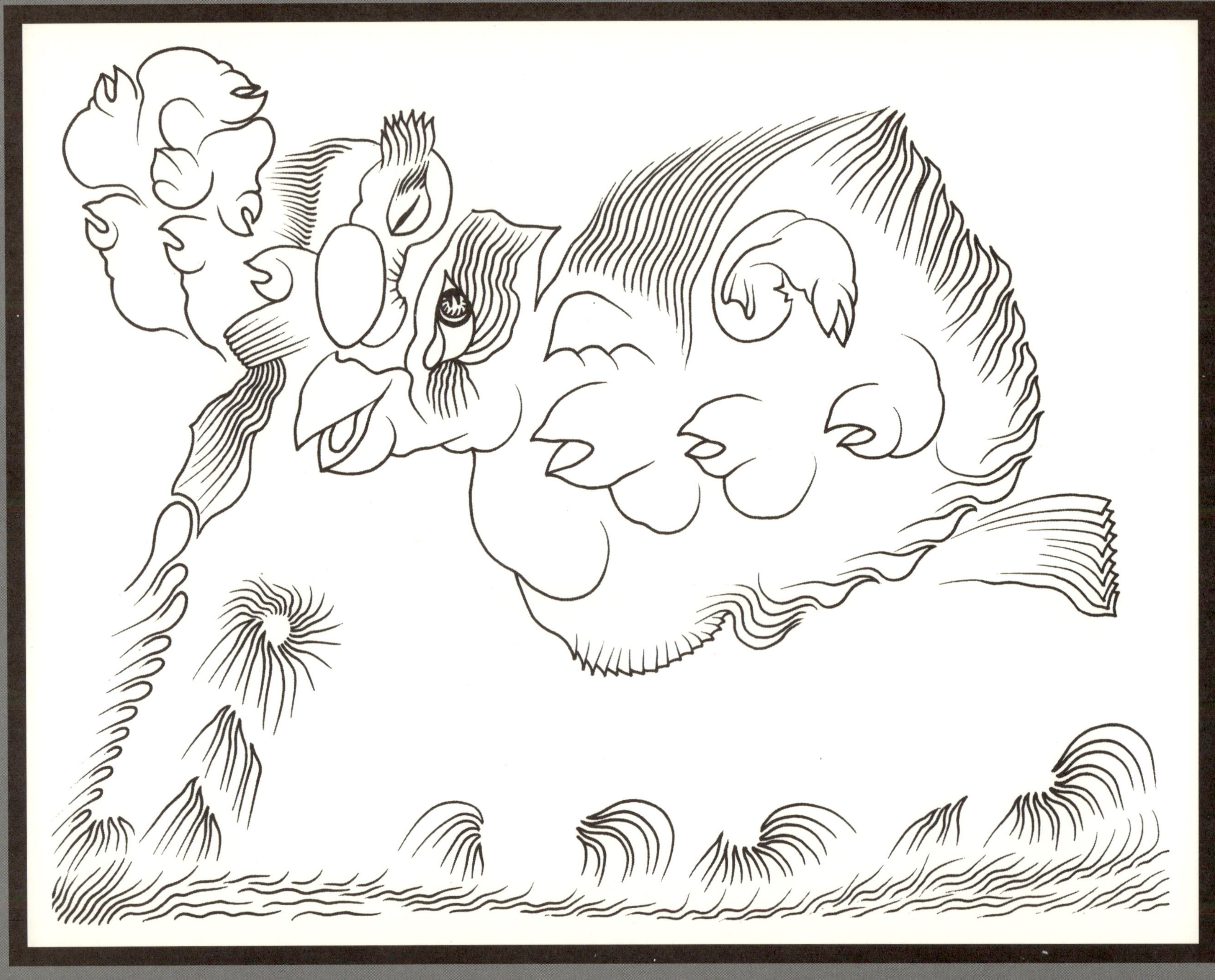

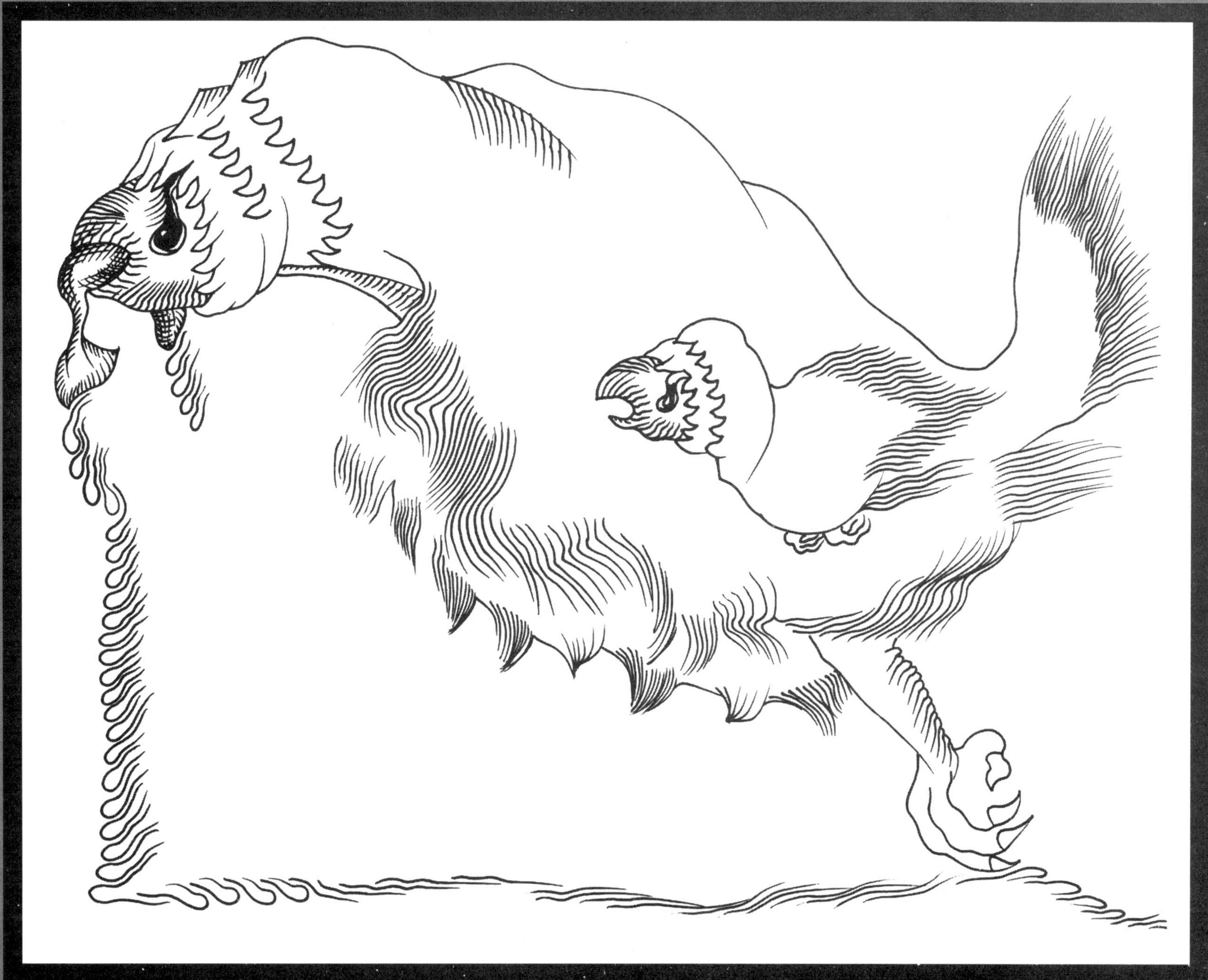

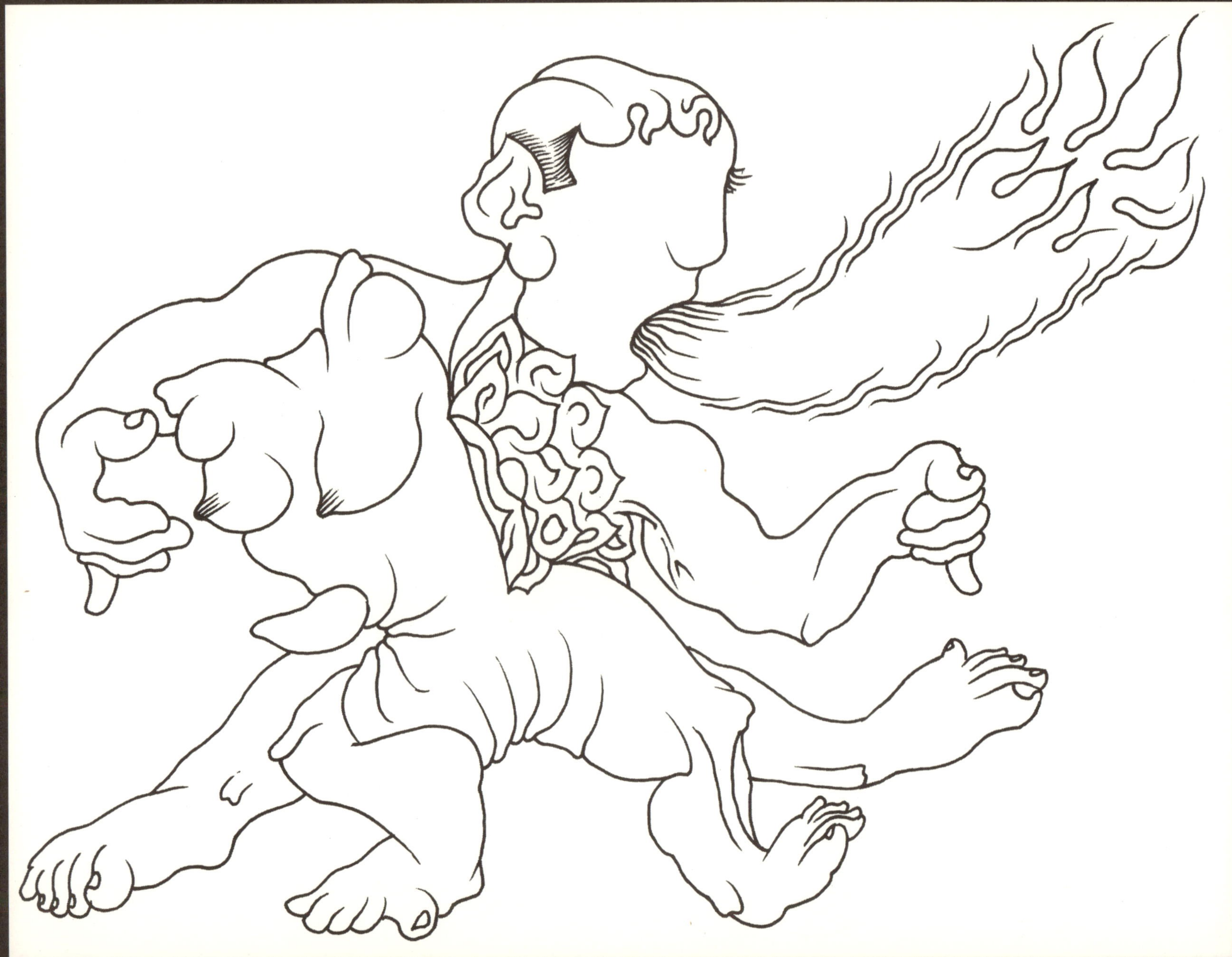

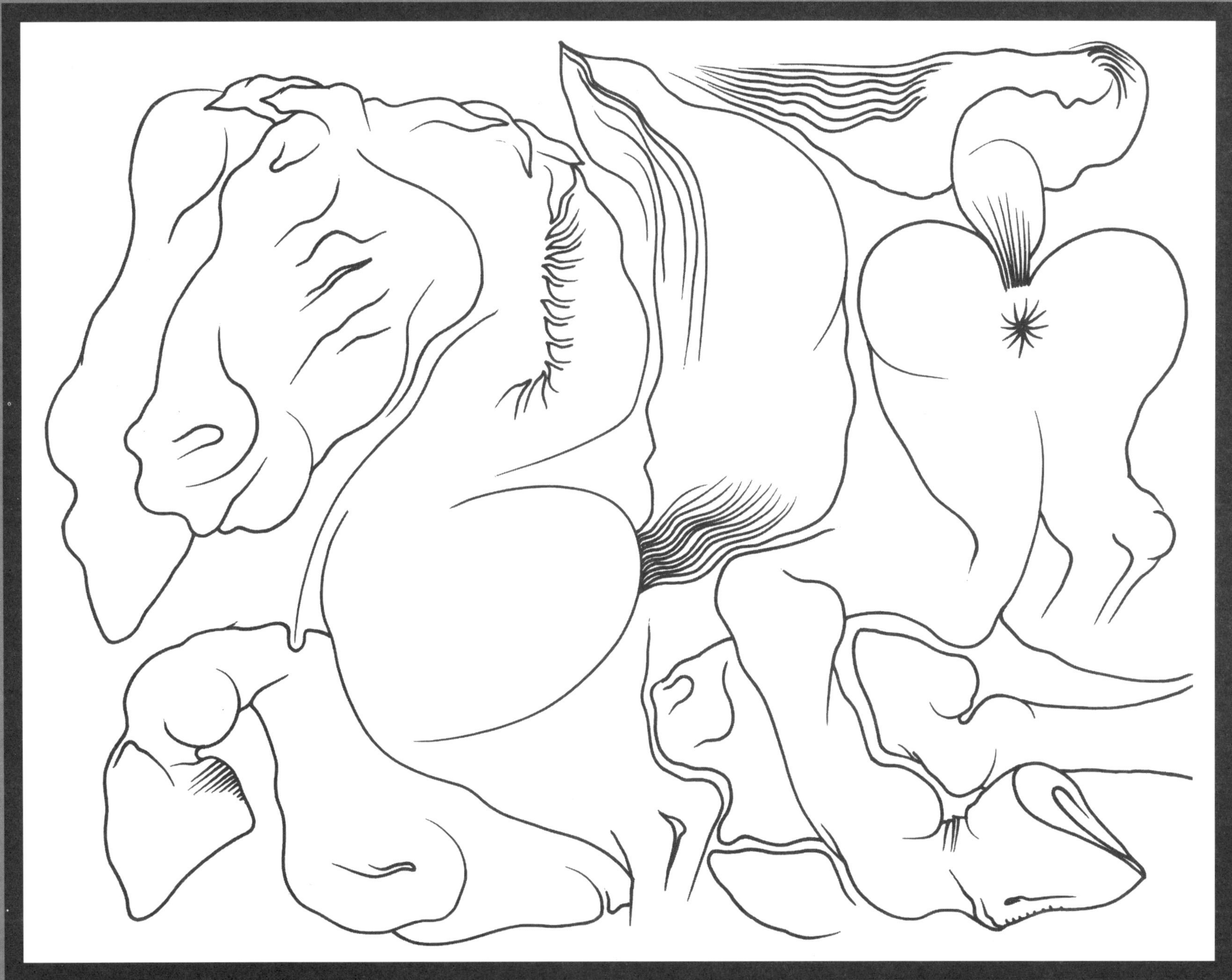

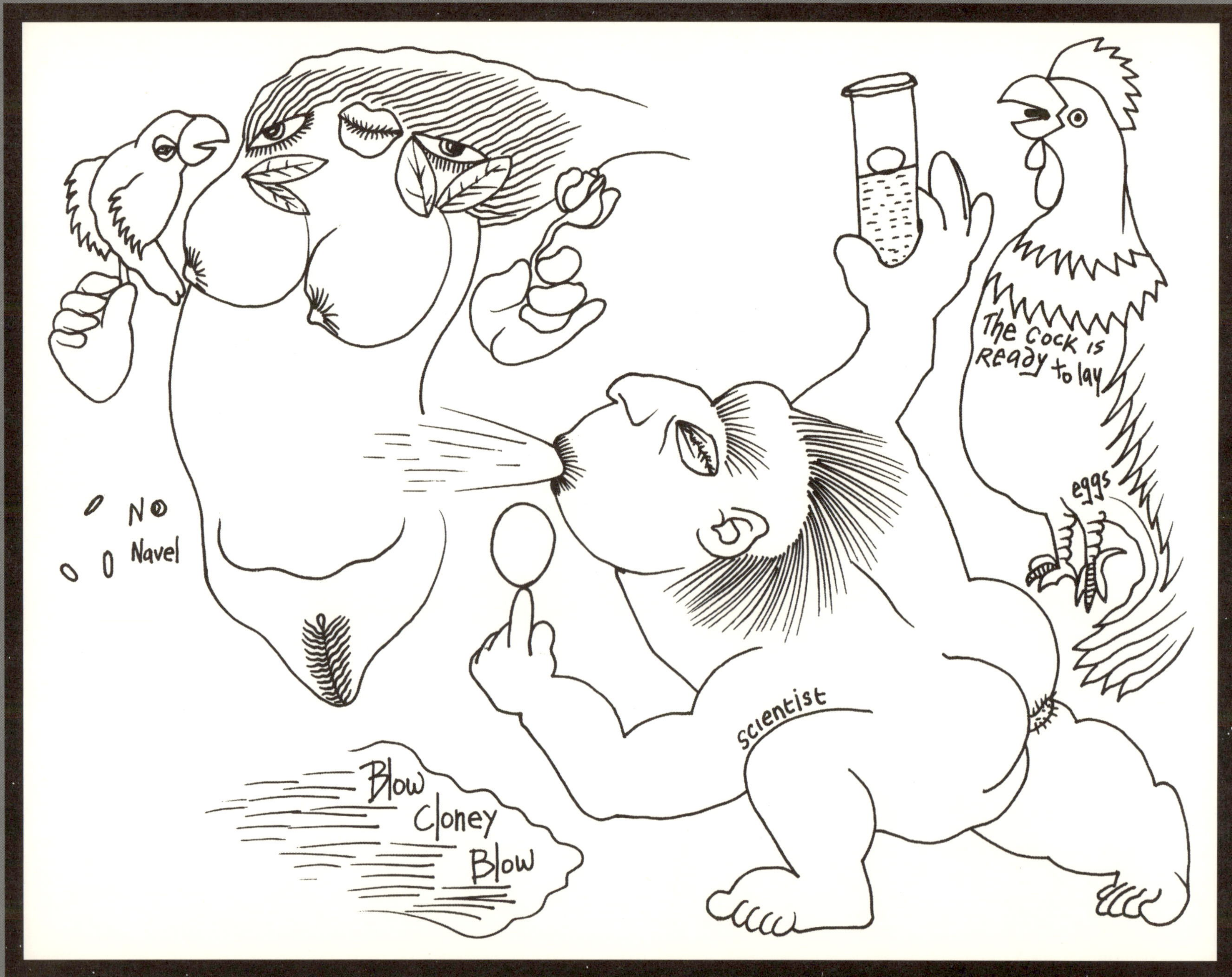
The cock is
Ready to lay
eggs
NO
Navel
scientist
Blow
Cloney
Blow

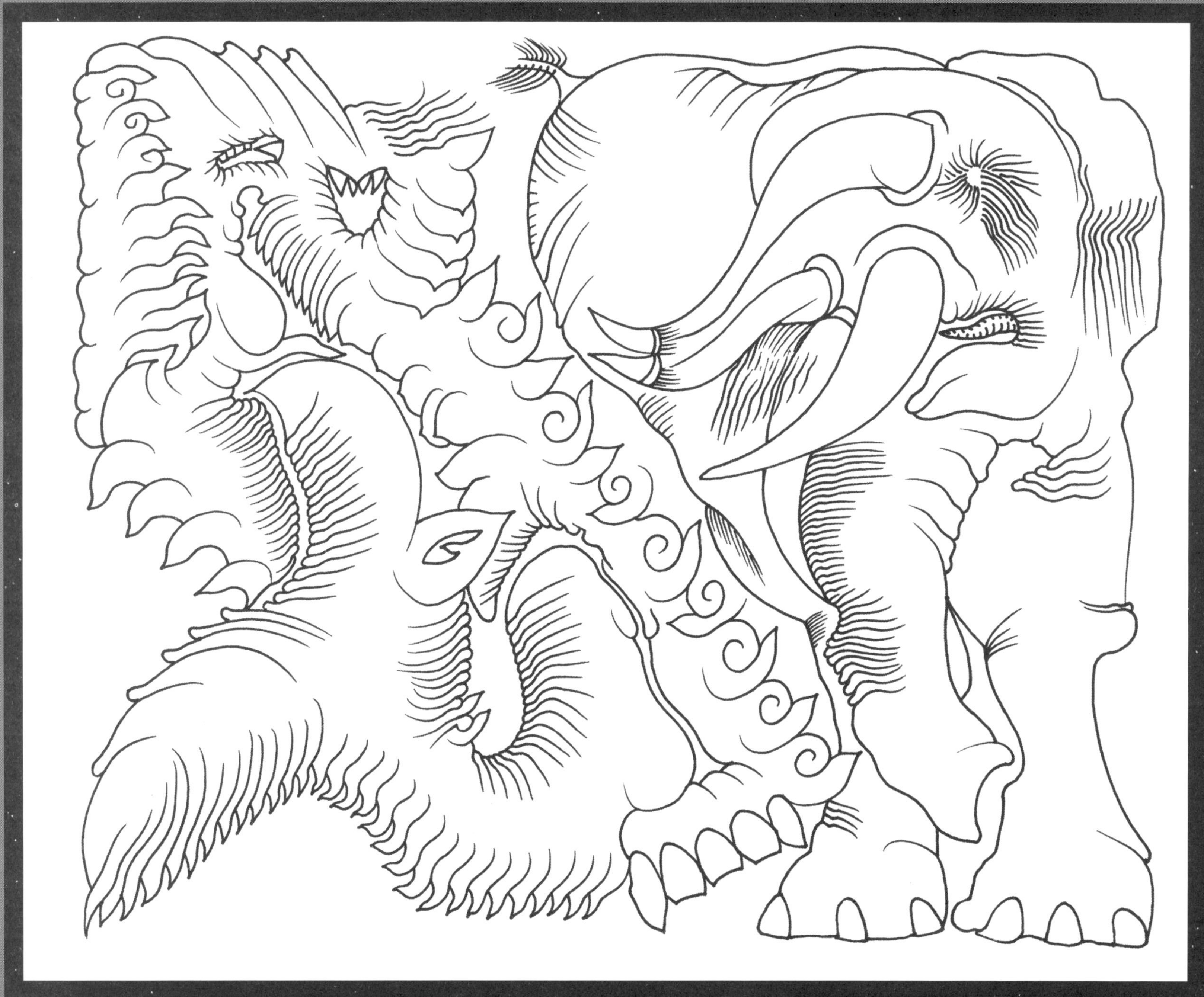

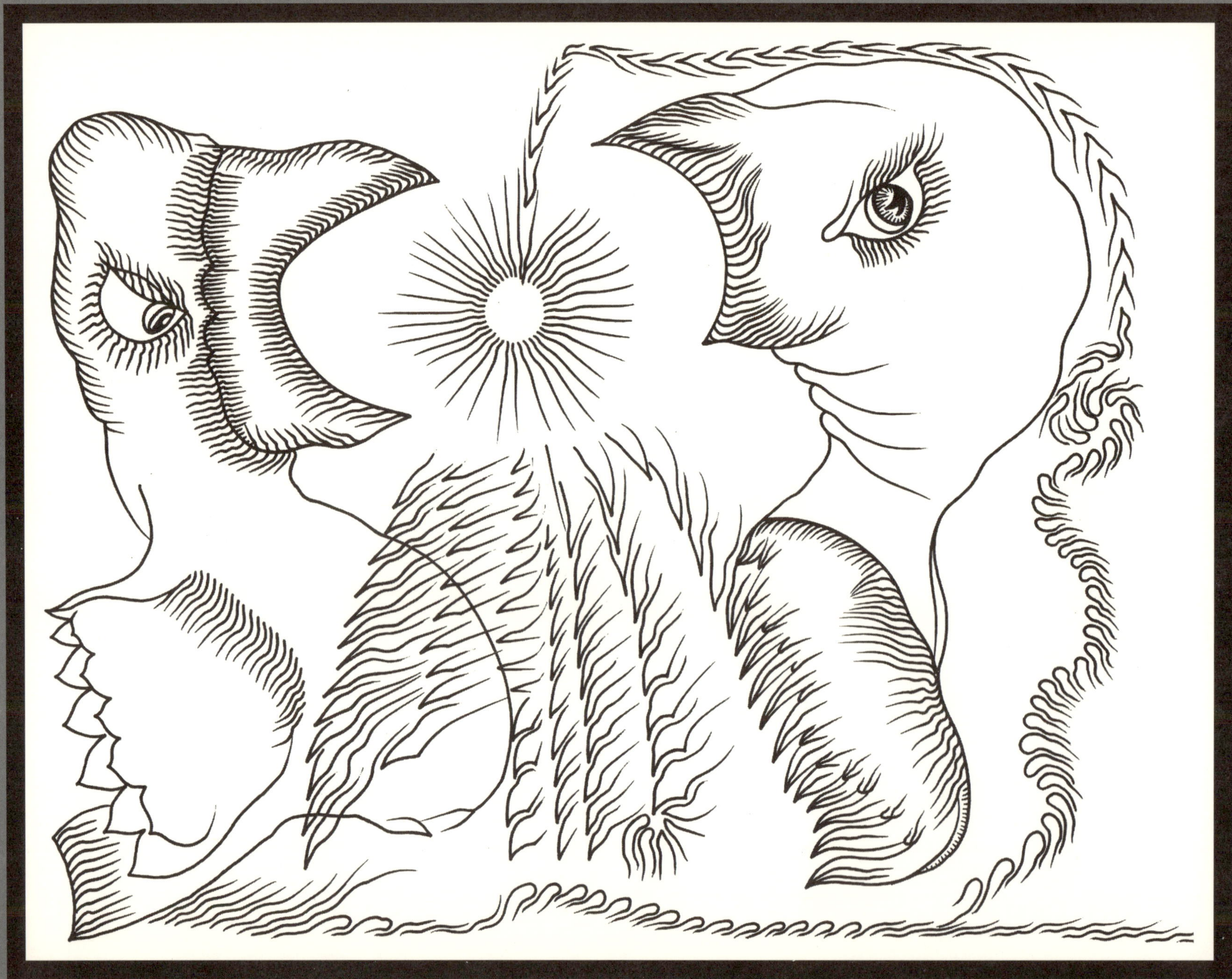

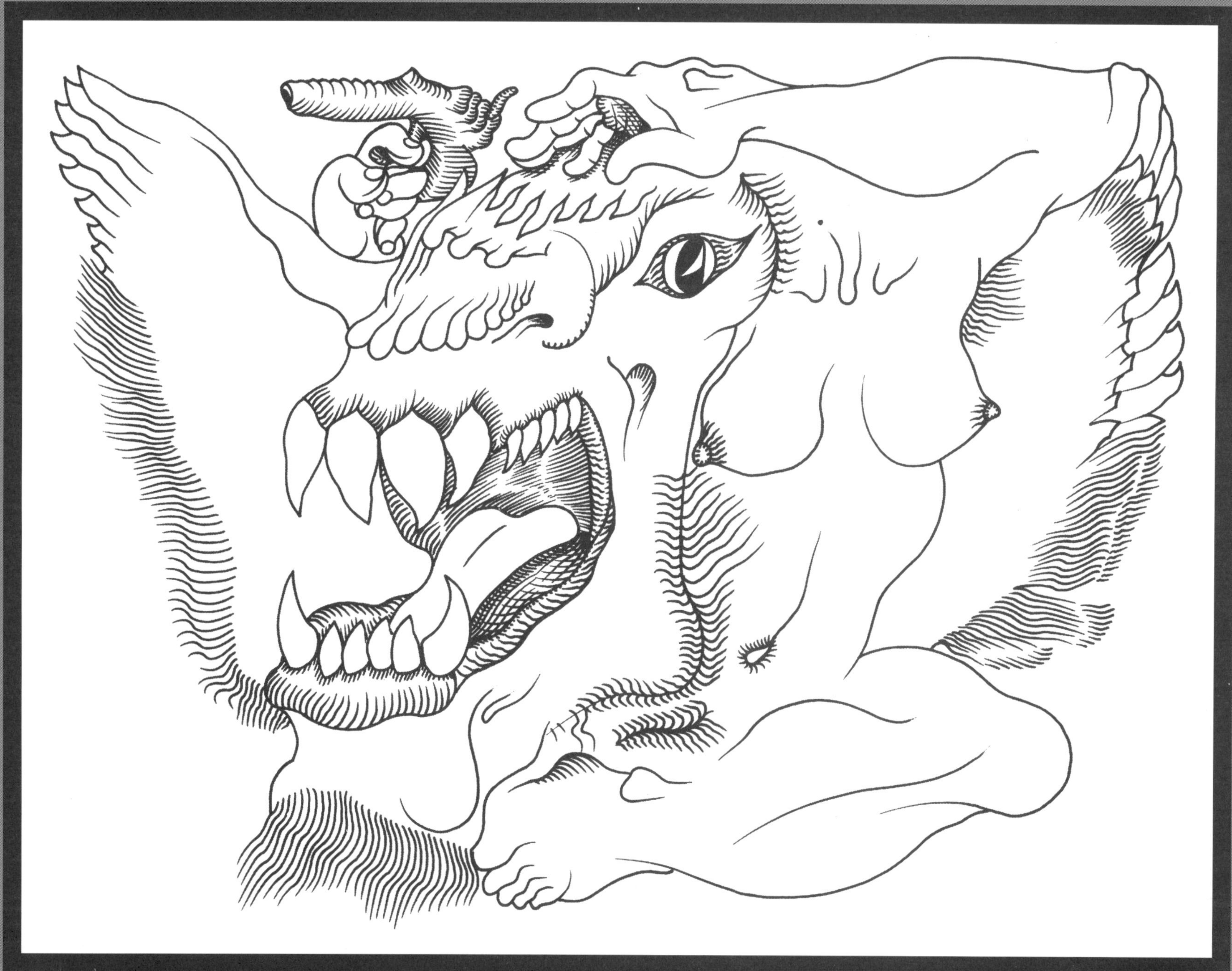

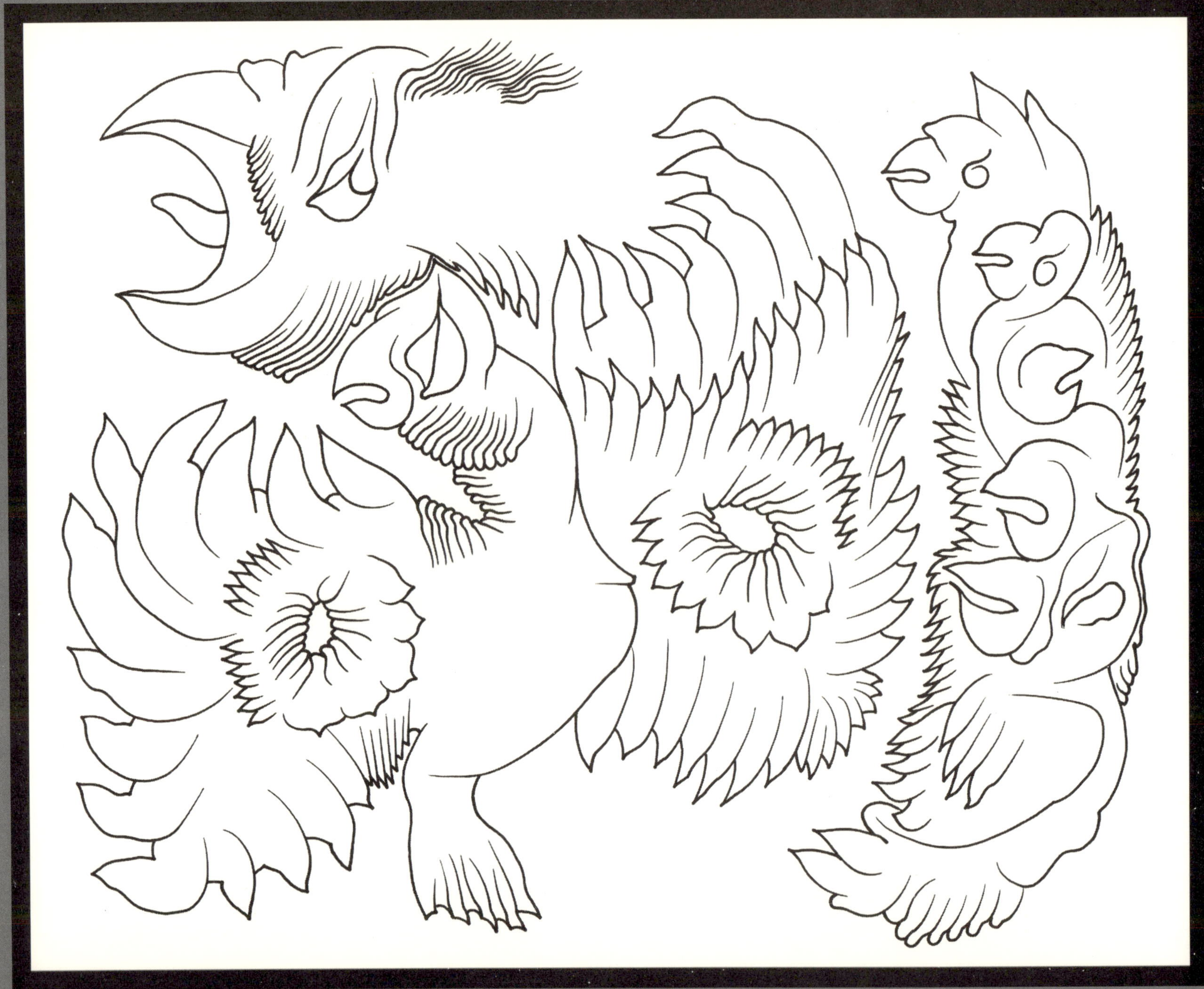

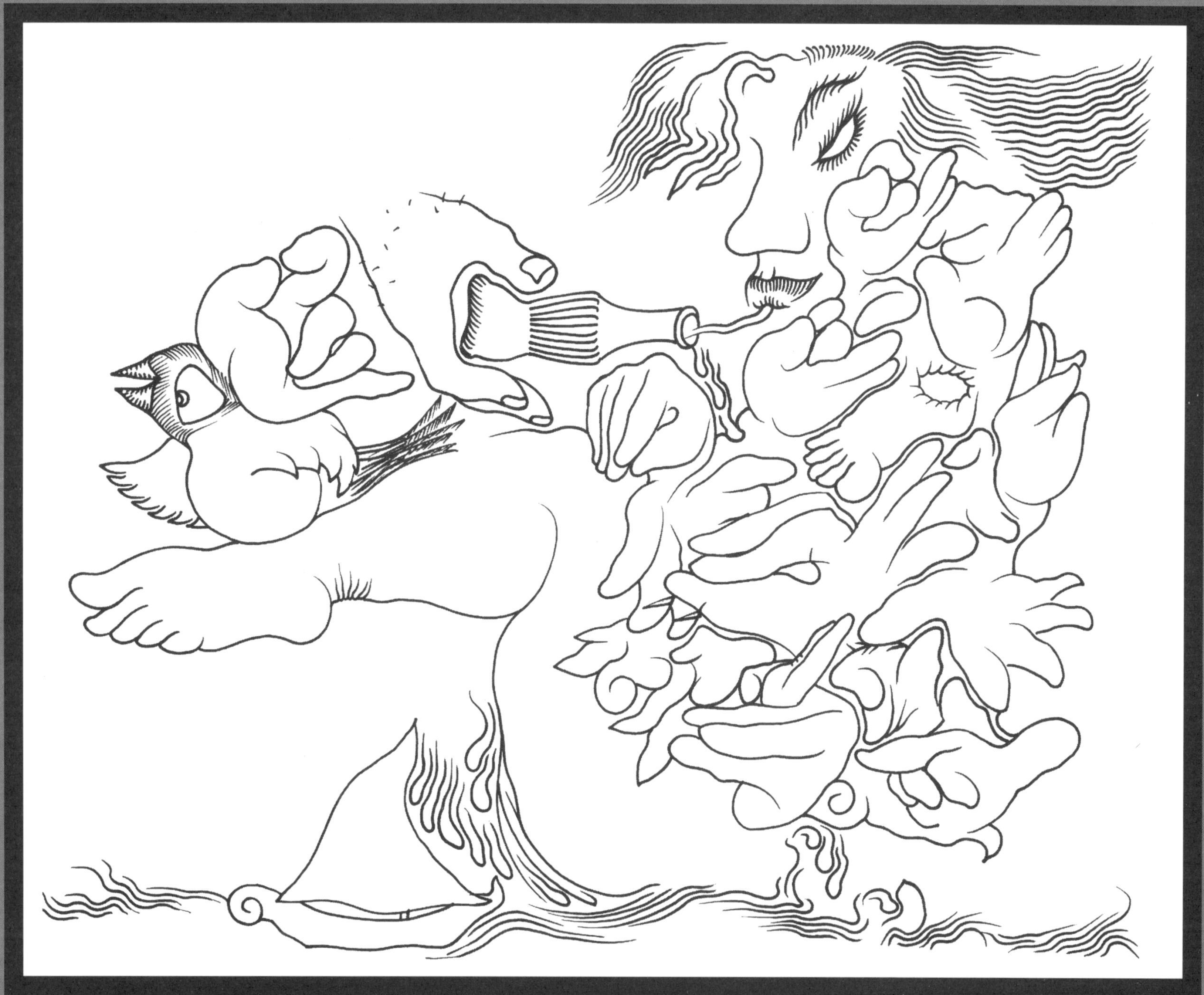

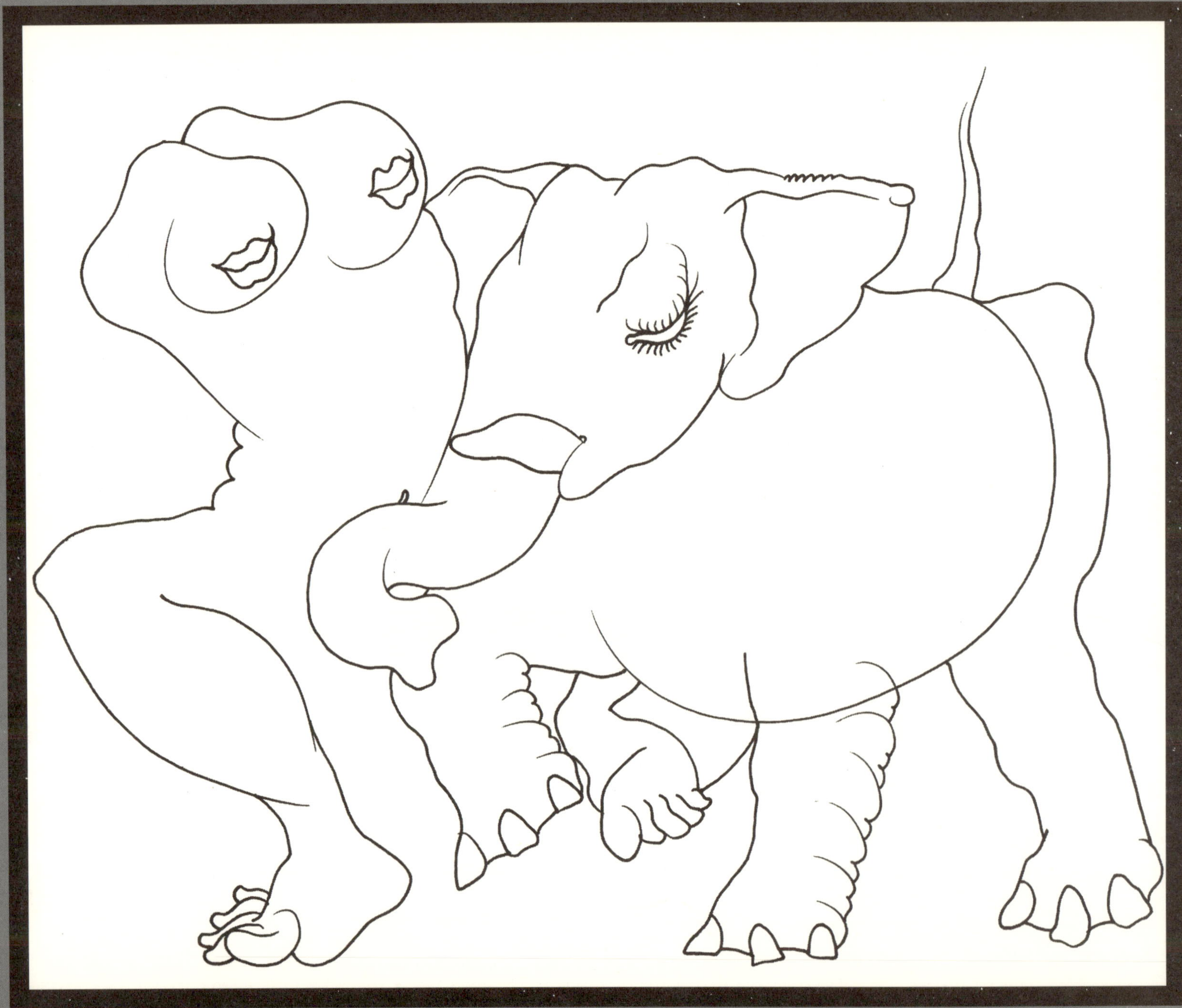

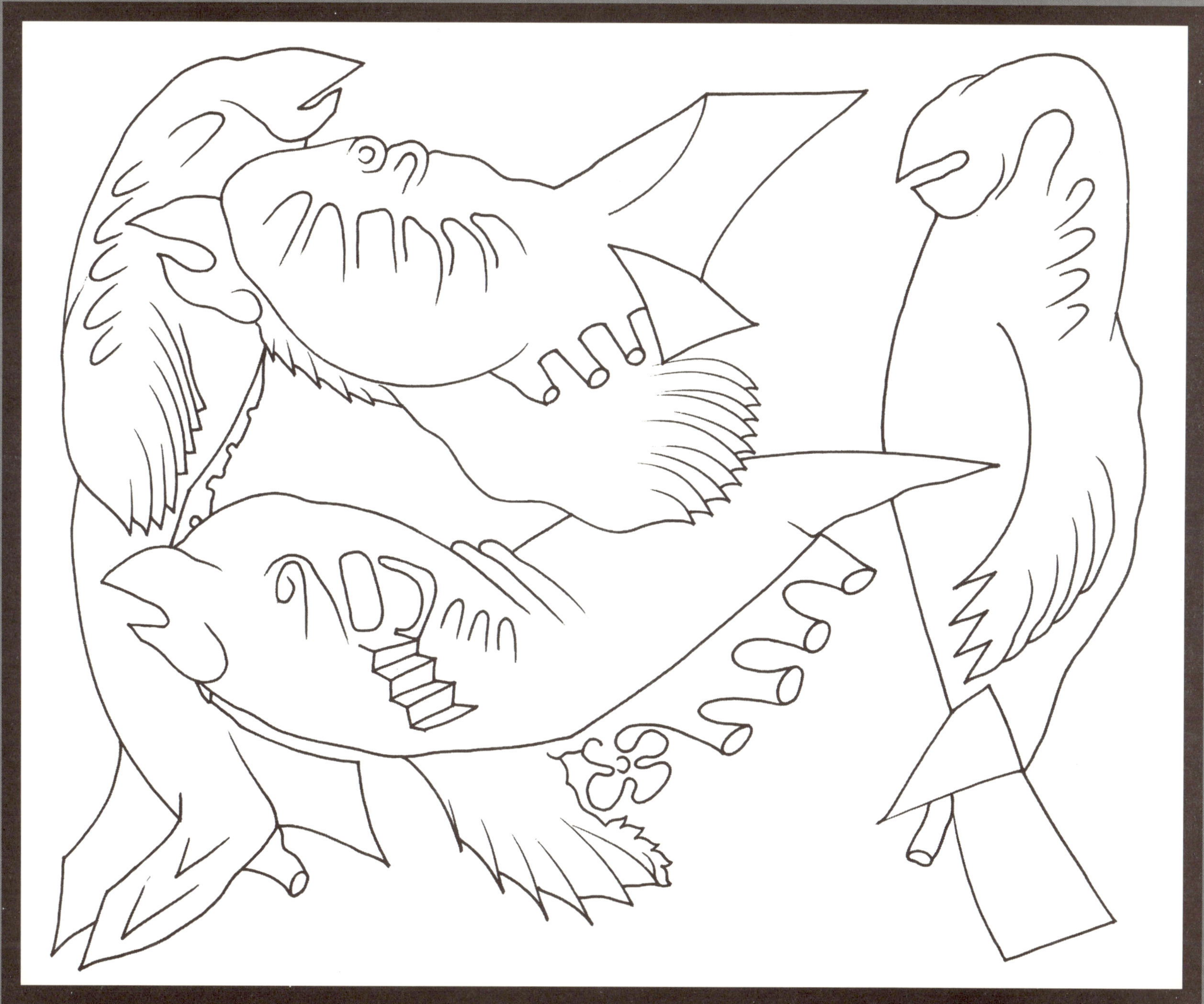

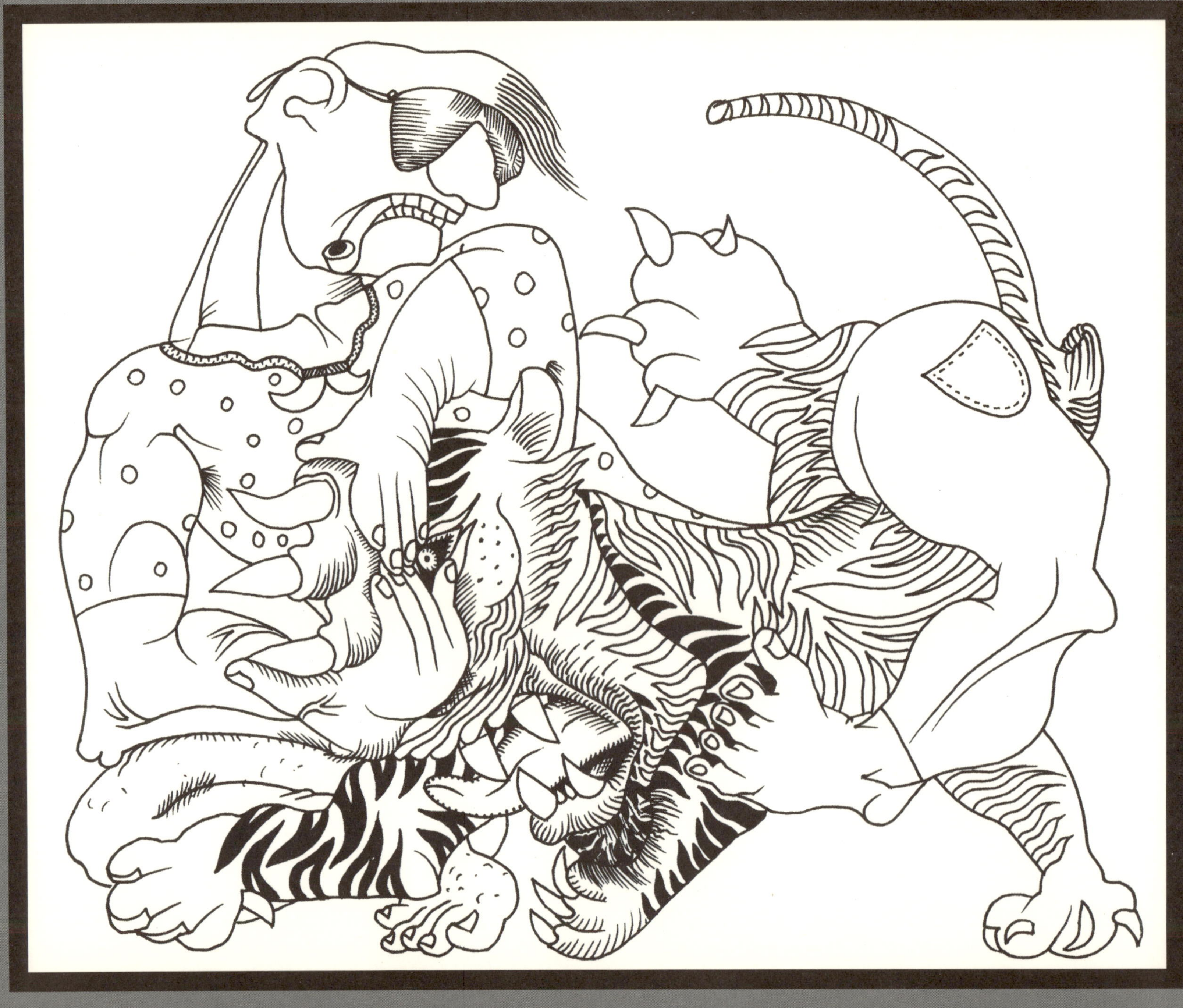

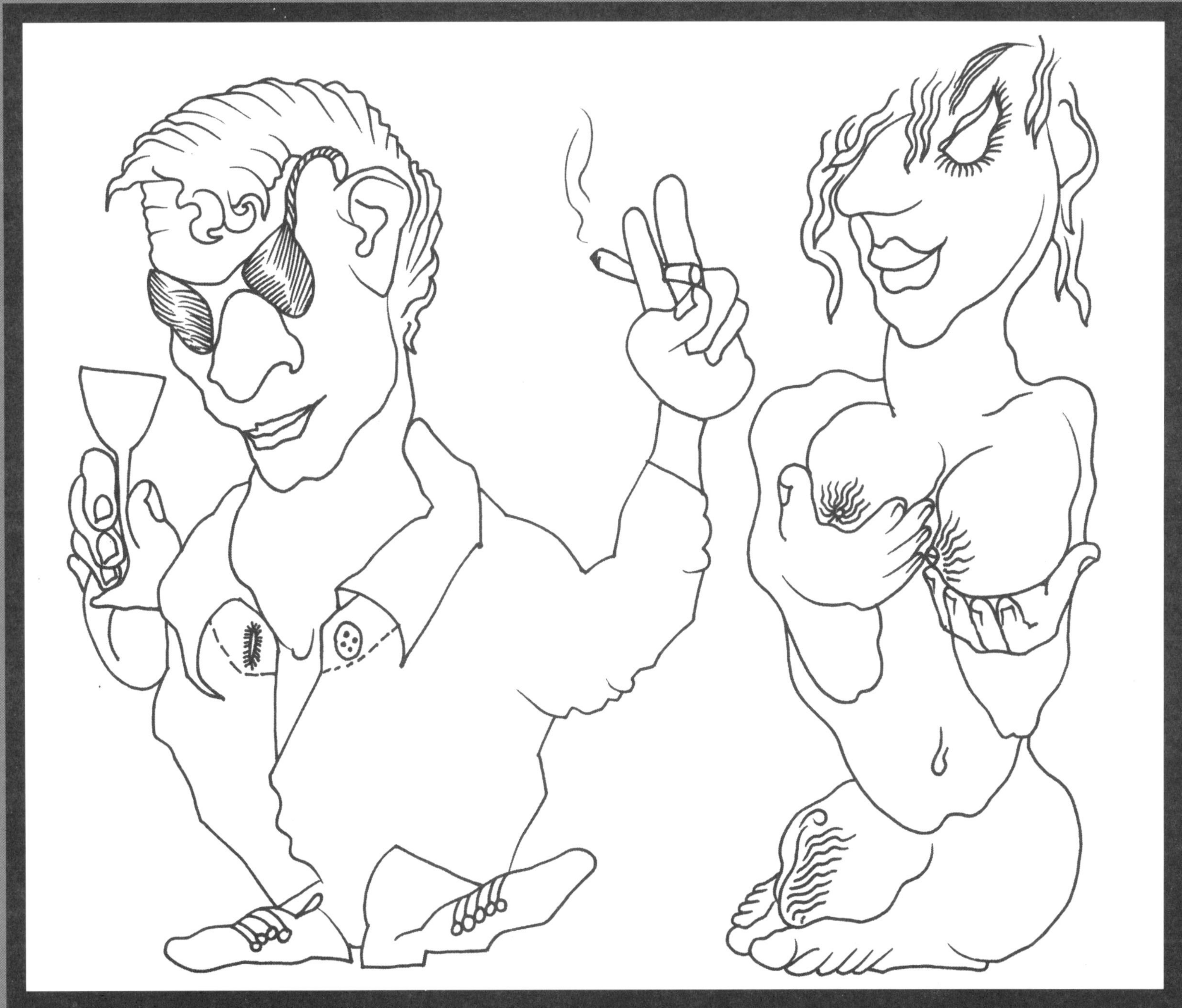

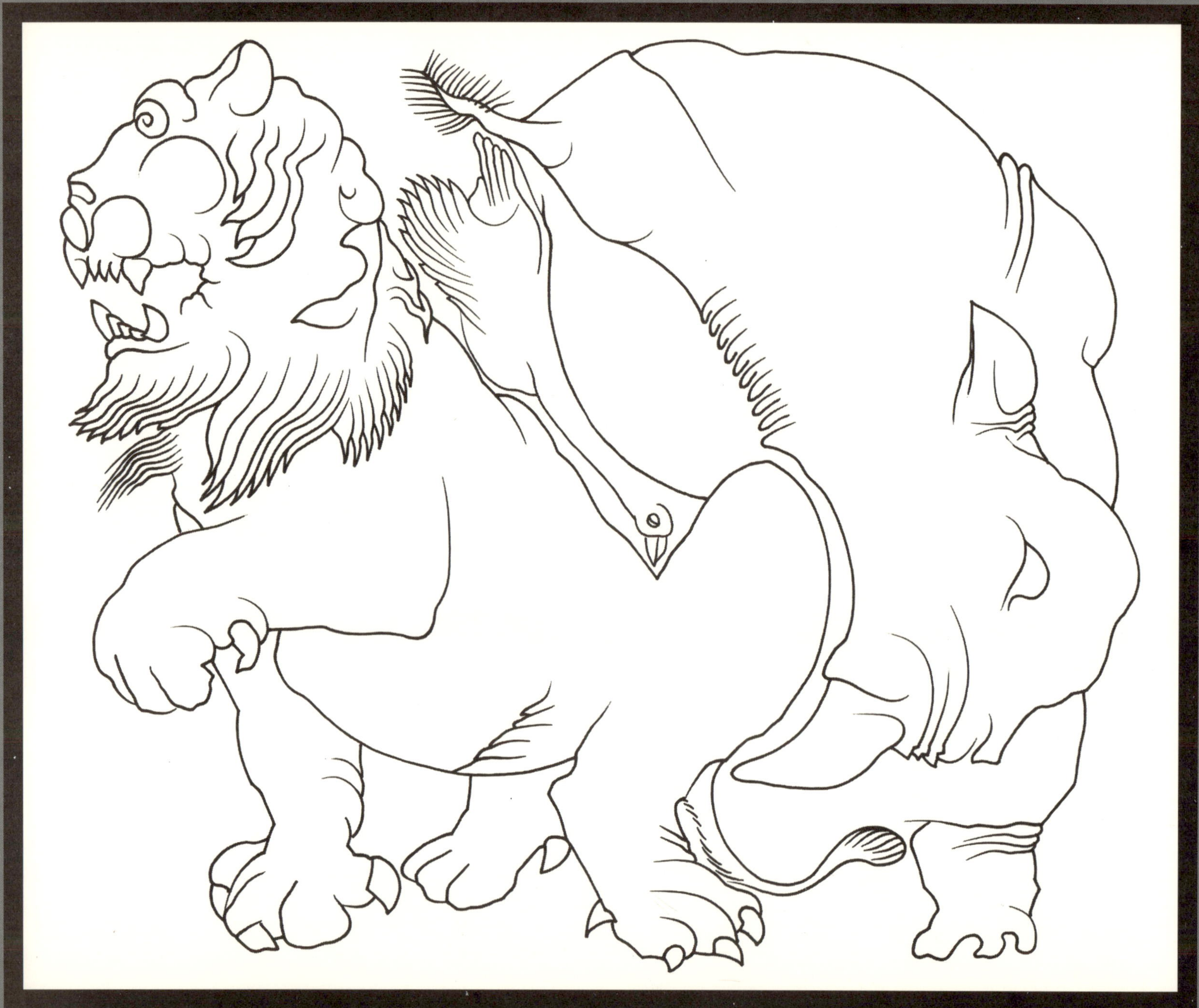

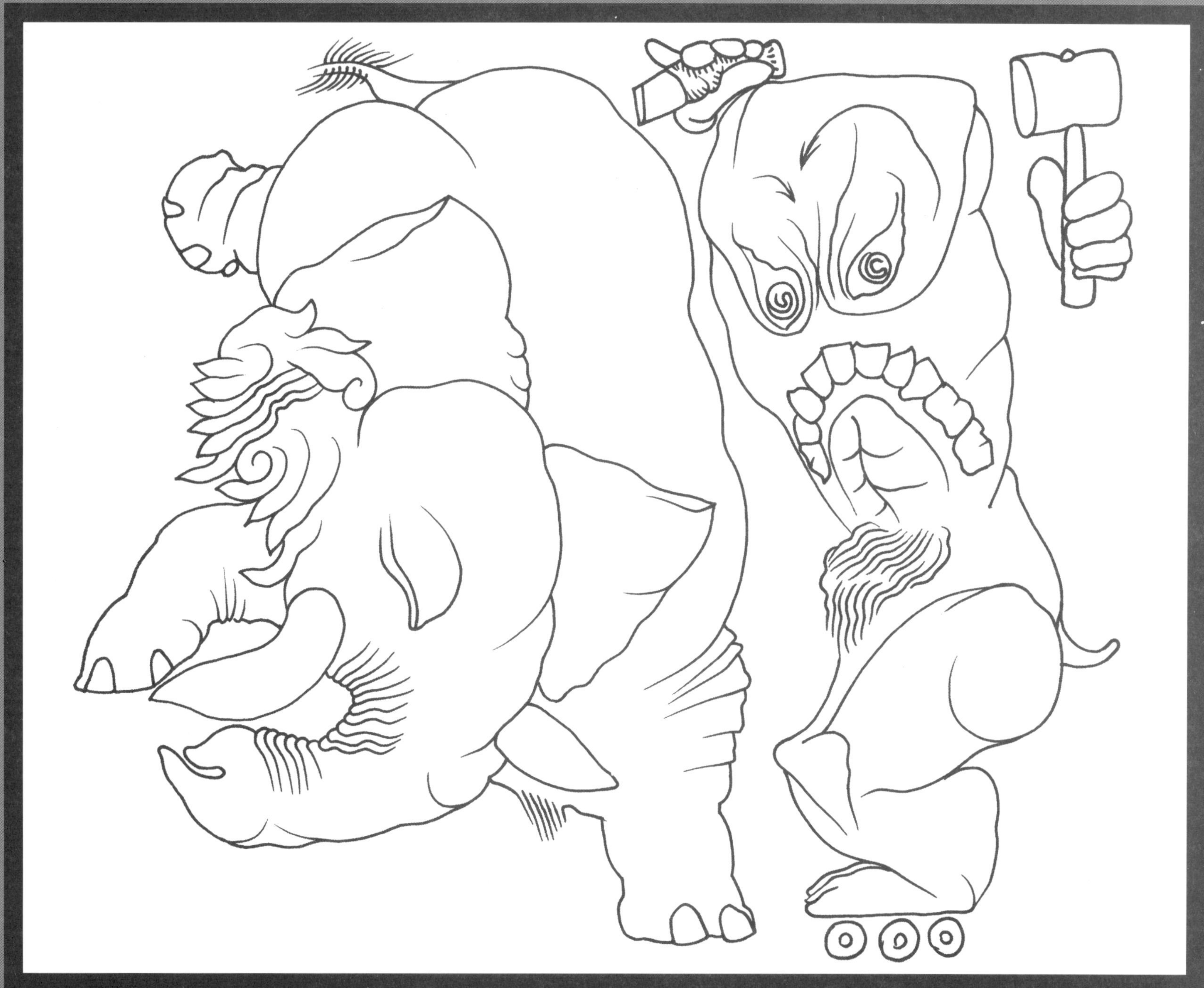

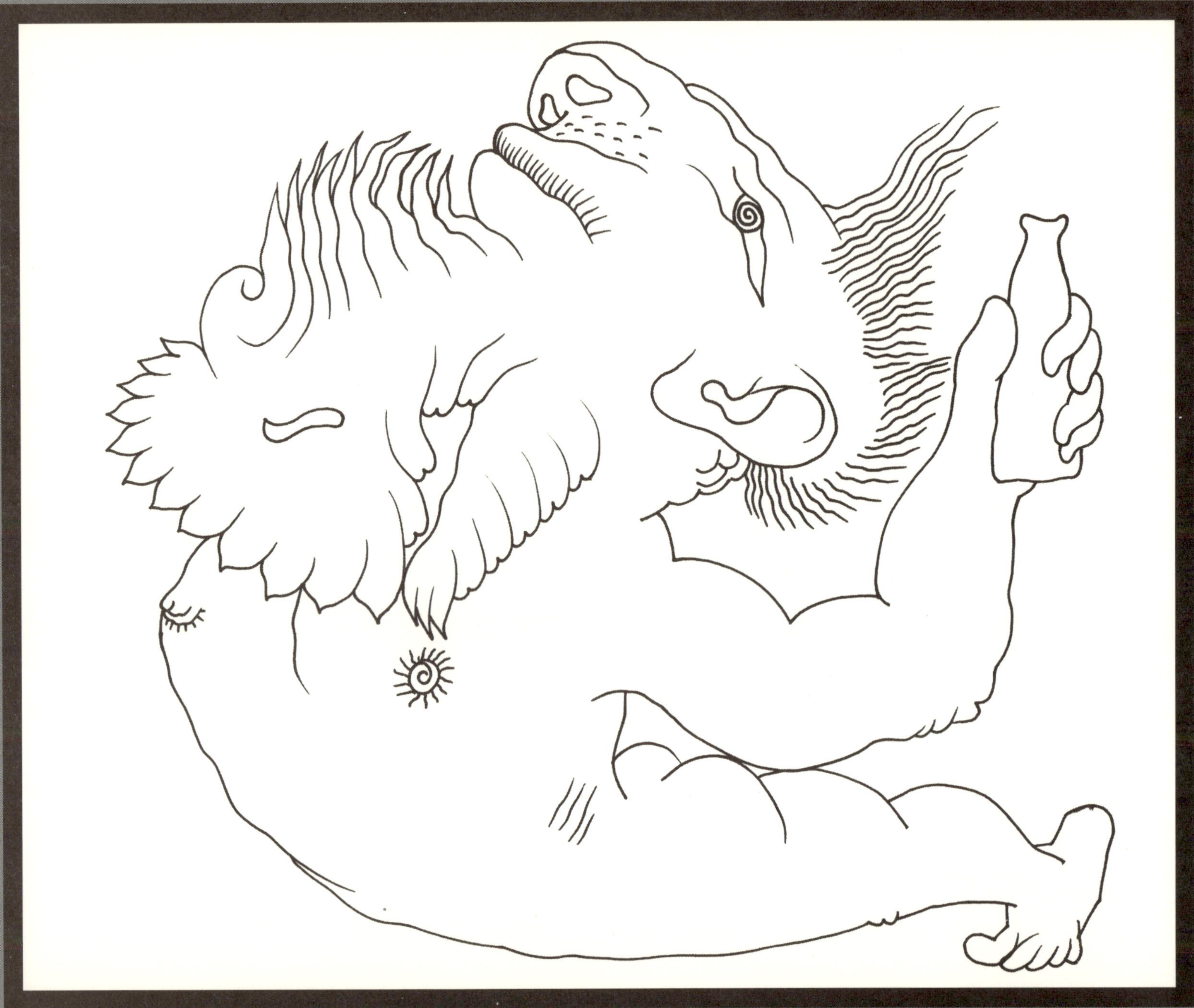

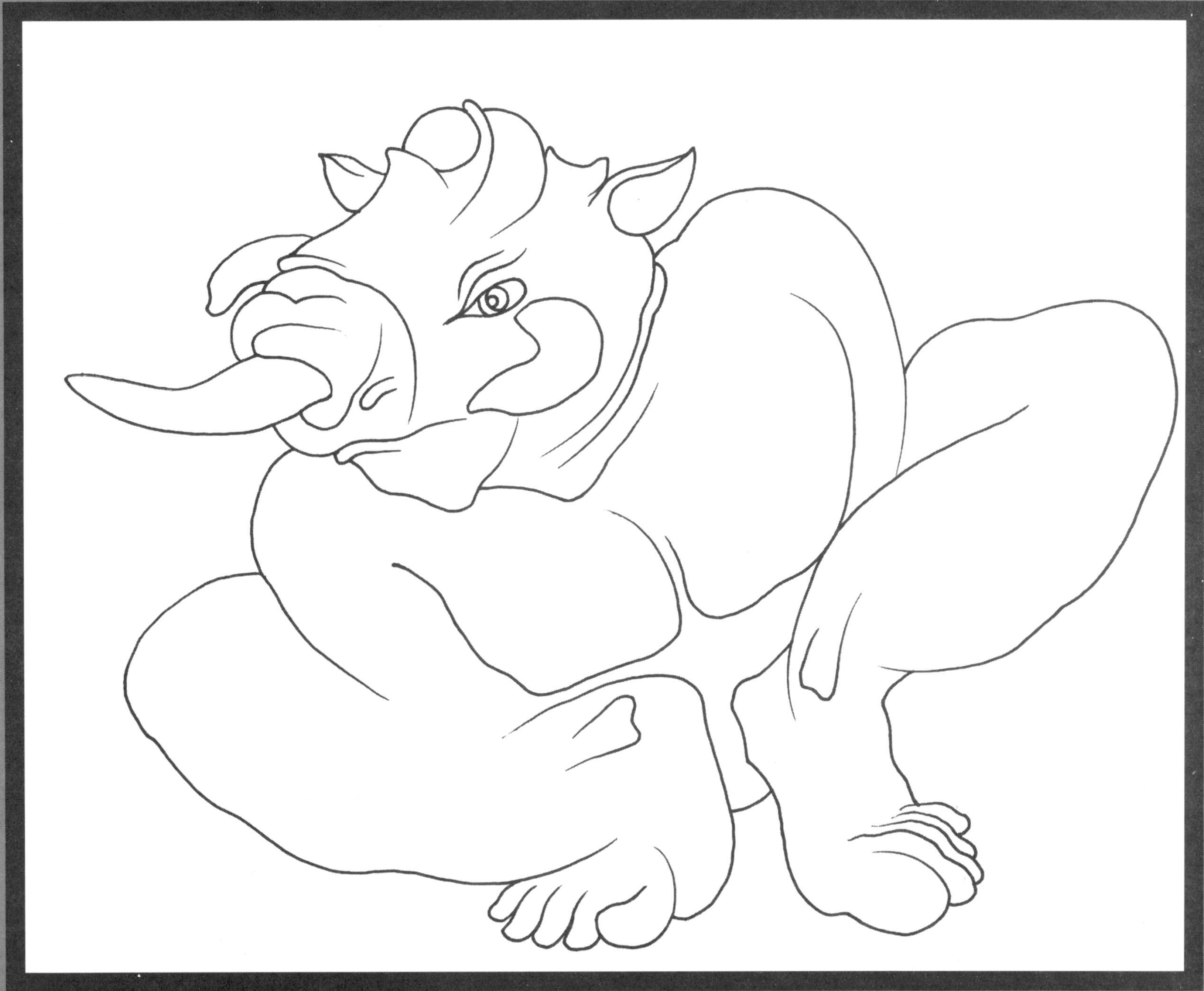

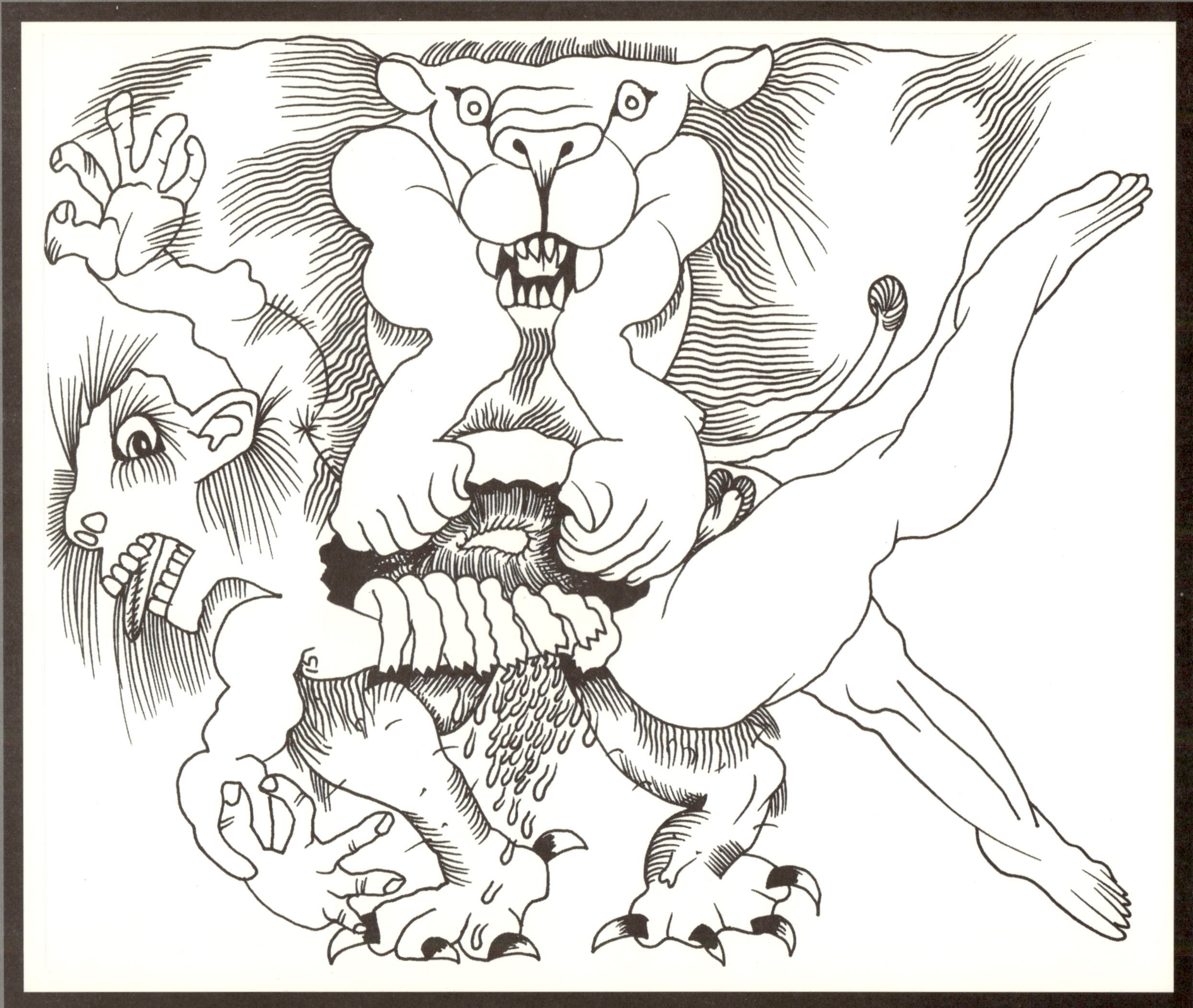

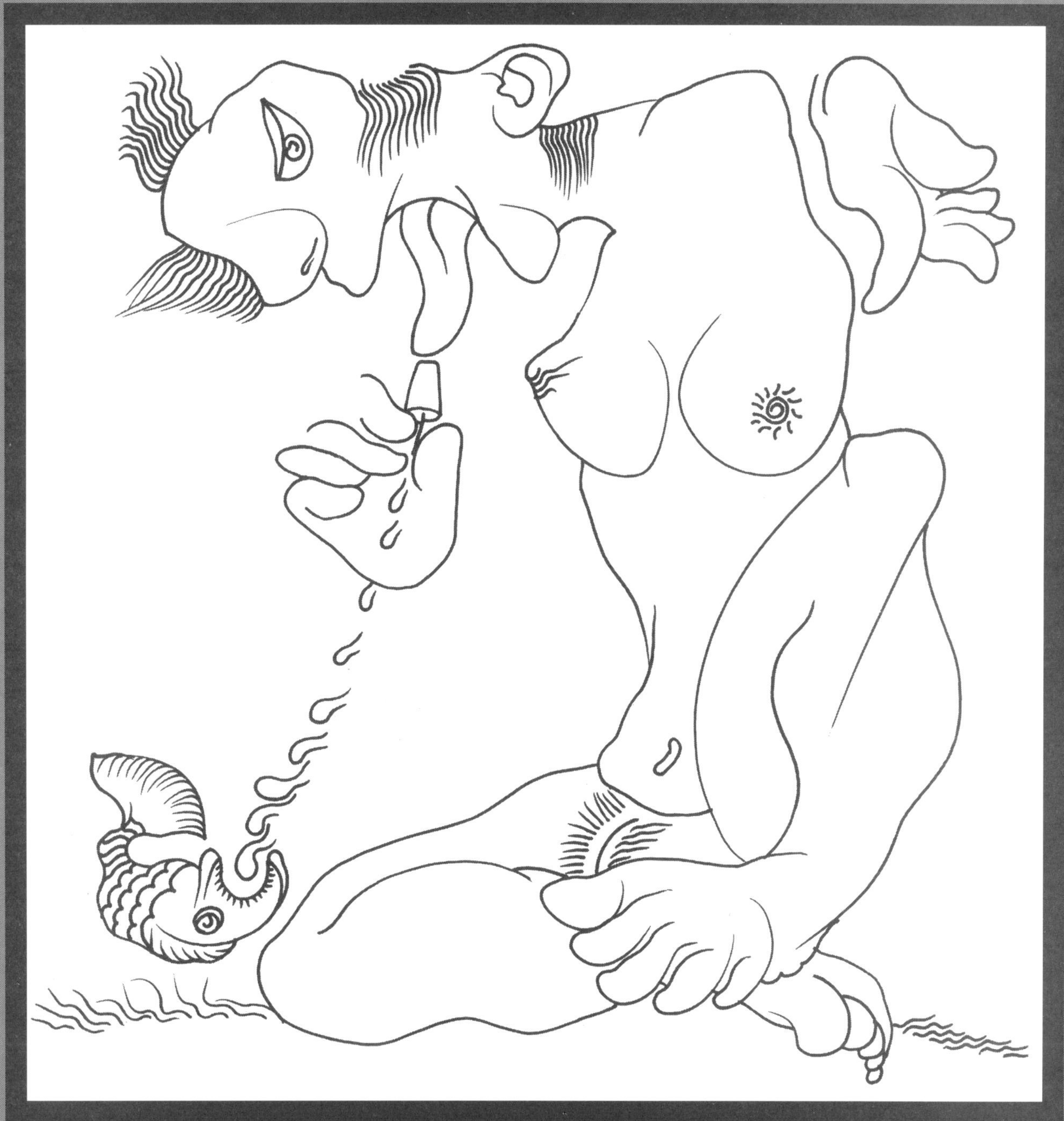

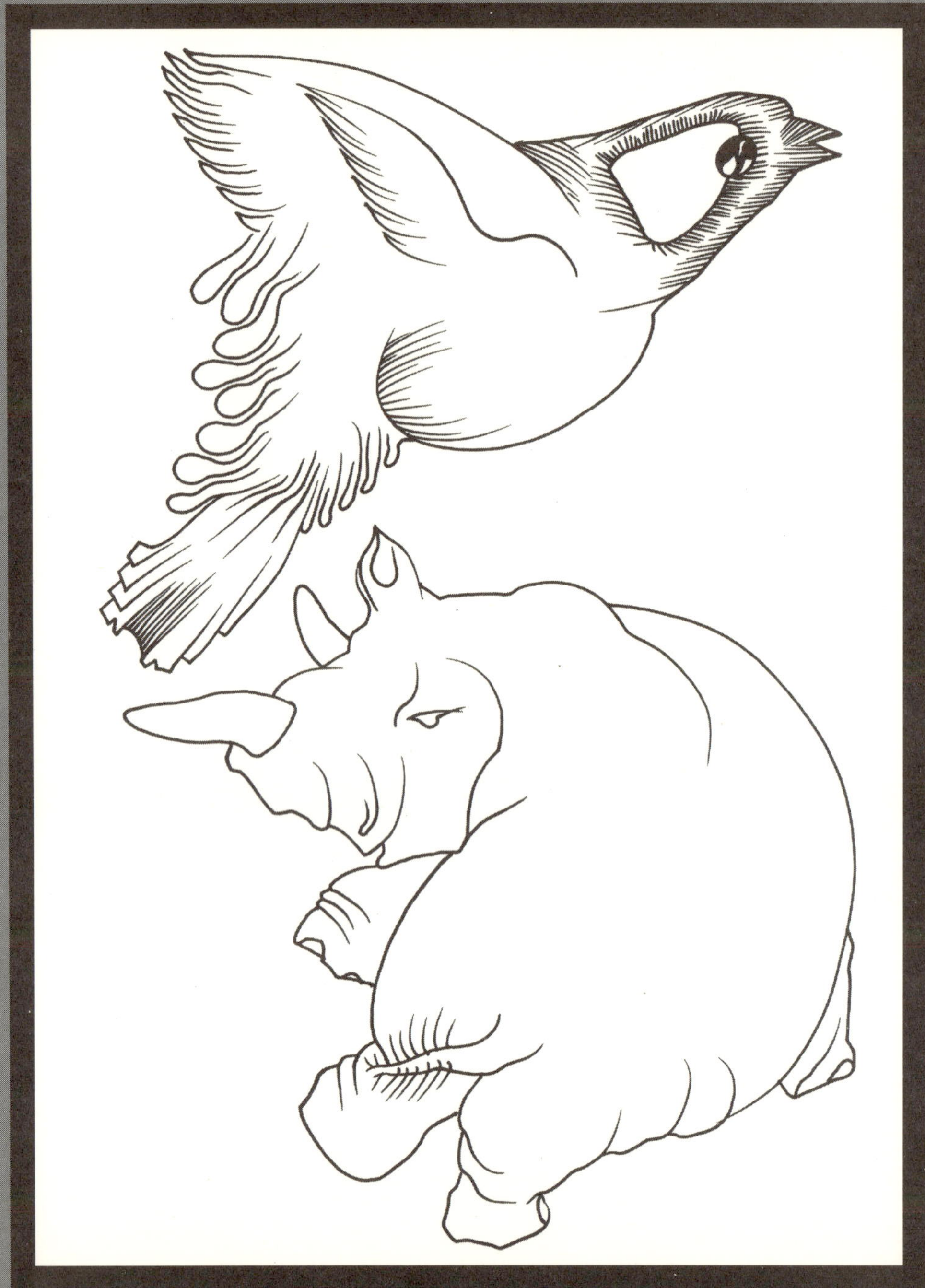

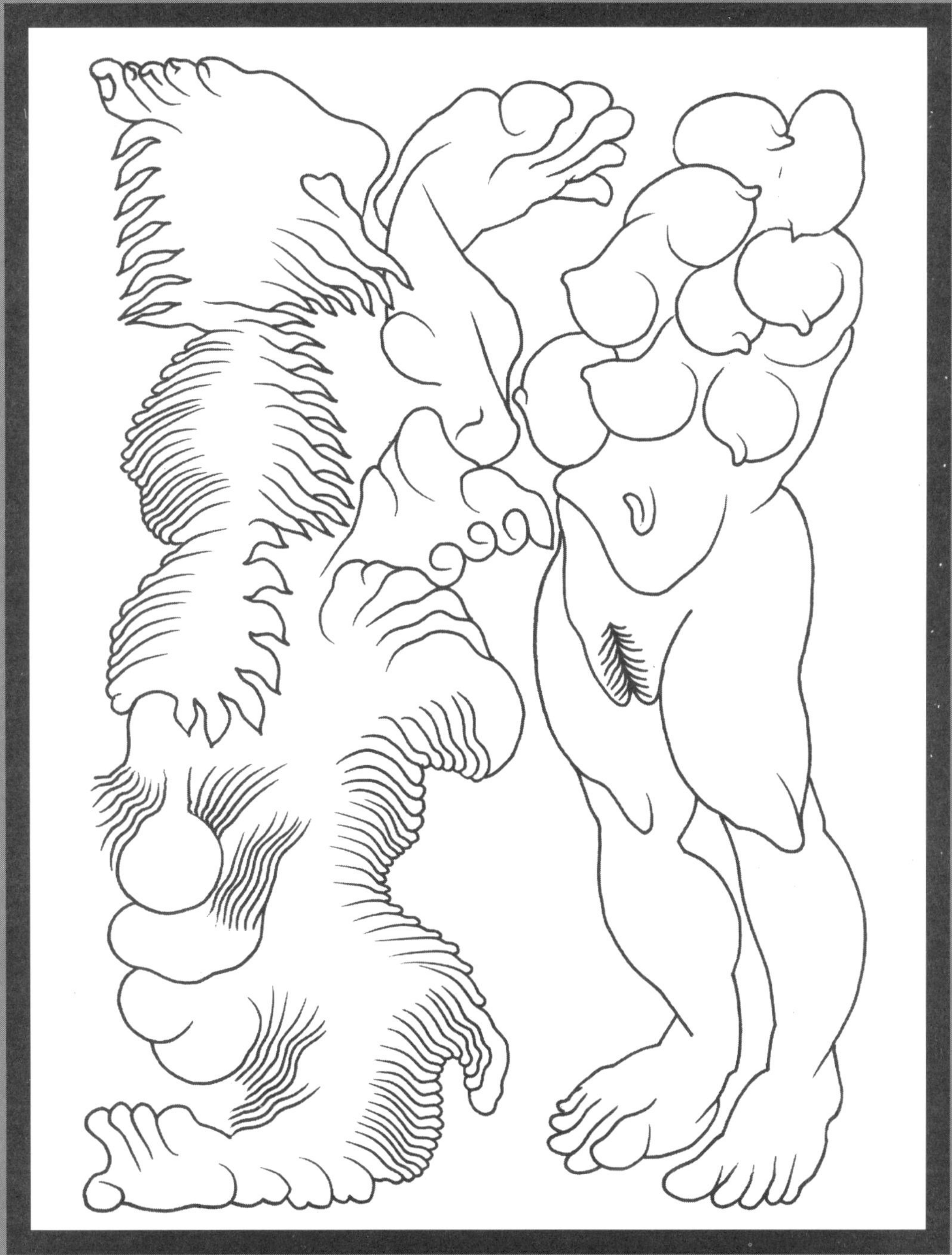

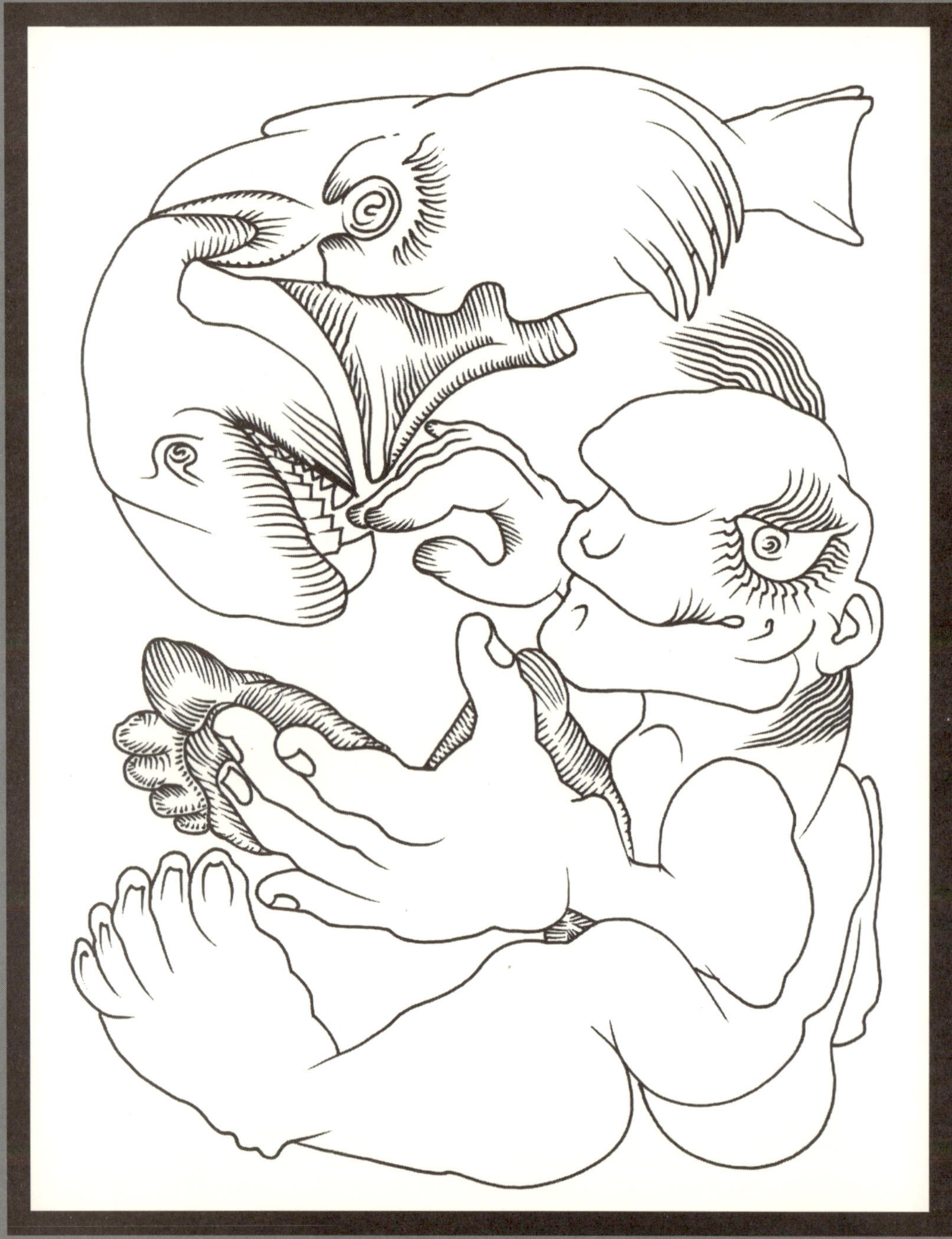

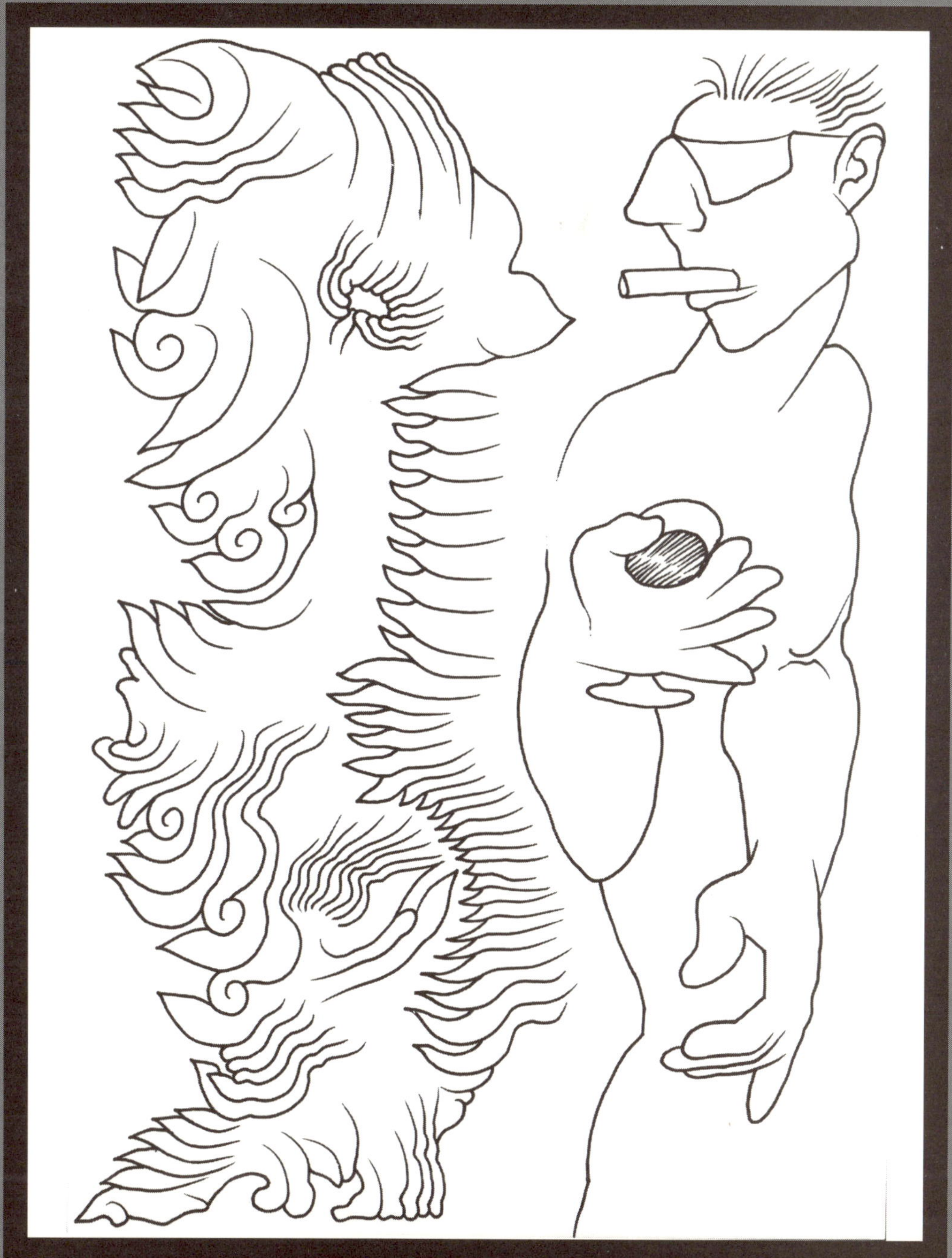

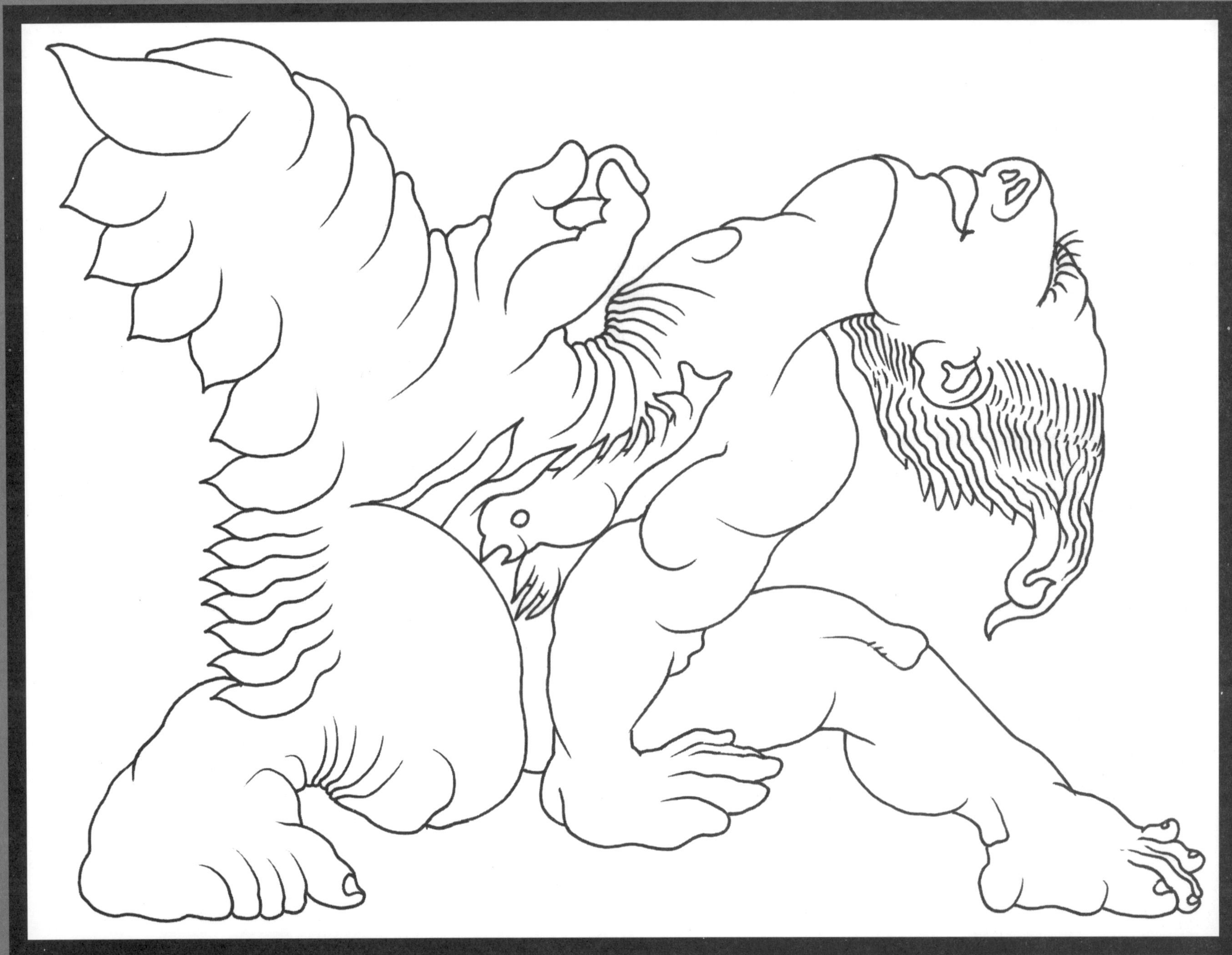

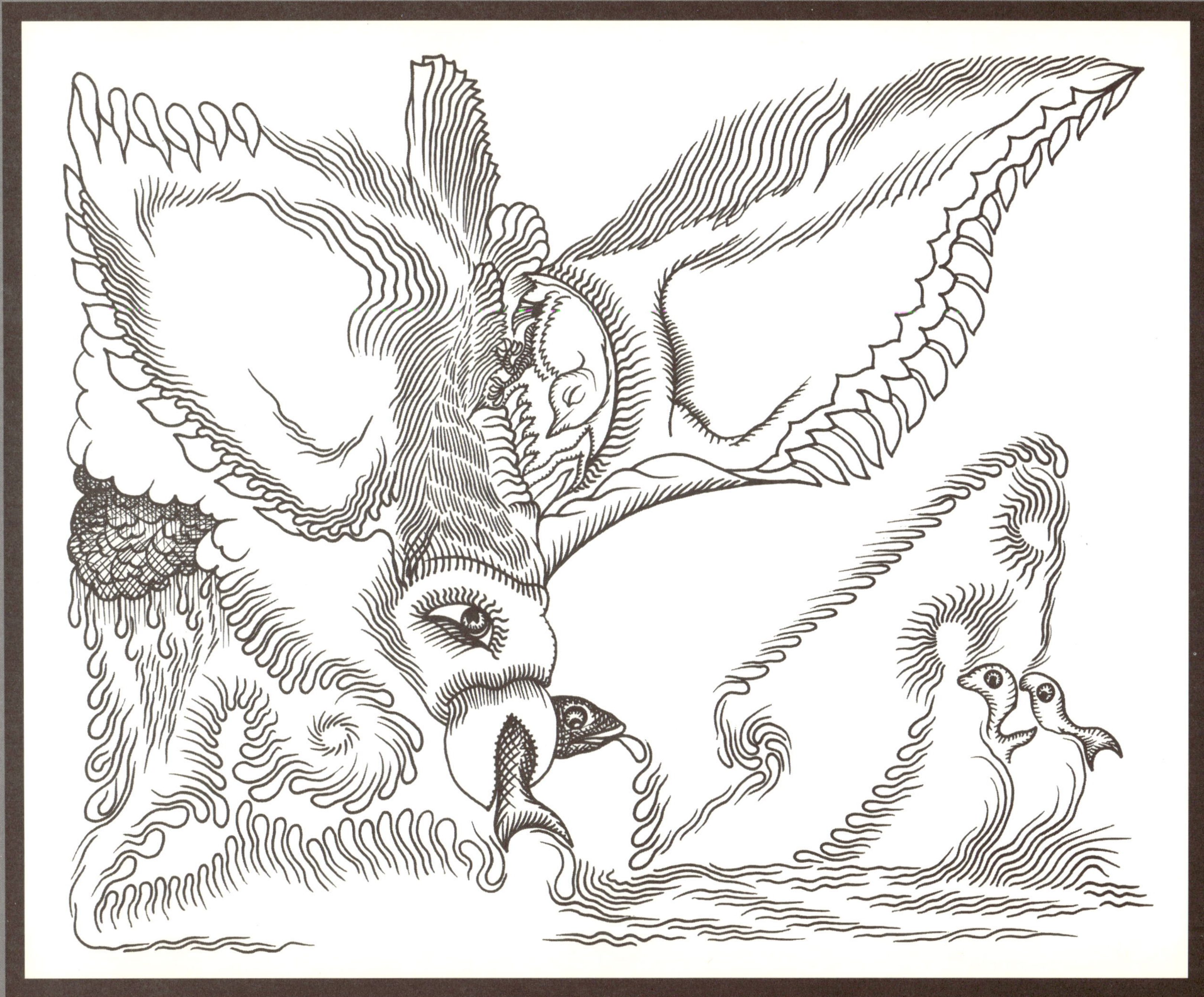

Natesh was born in 1960 in Chennai, India's cultural capital. He studied at the Madras Government College of Arts and Crafts and also learned printmaking and serigraphy under the tutelage of British printmakers. He has had numerous solo shows of his paintings, drawings, and installation art in Chennai, Pondichery, Mumbai, Delhi, and La Gerulde, France.

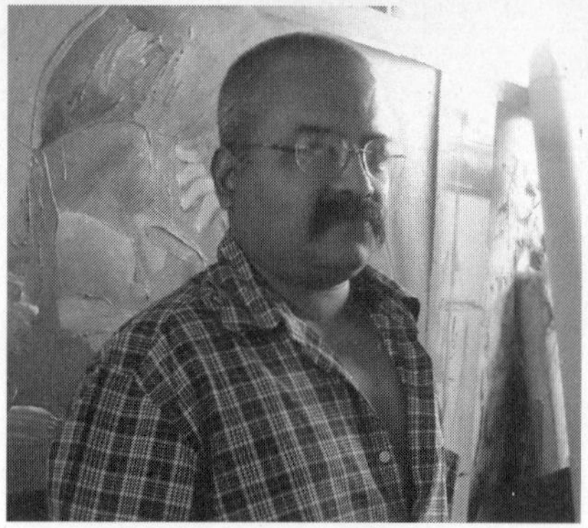

He is also an accomplished set and lighting designer in the experimental performing arts scene. He has built sets and designed lighting for the legendary choreographer Chandralekha, for Pandit Ravi Shankar's dance/theatre production *Ganashyam*, and for numerous English and Tamil theatre productions in Chennai.

www.rajunatesh.com
rajunatesh@gmail.com